Safe Sanctuaries for Ministers

Best Practices and Ethical Decisions

Joy Thornburg Melton

DISCIPLESHIP RESOURCES

P.O. BOX 340003 • NASHVILLE, TN 37203-0003
www.discipleshipresources.org

Dedication

This book is dedicated to J. Lloyd Knox, retired Bishop of the United Methodist Church. Bishop Knox has demonstrated his devotion to excellence, integrity, honesty, and trustworthiness throughout his career in ministry. He has been a persistent advocate for building Safe Sanctuaries® in ministry through building the ethical decision-making abilities of the clergy and their parishioners. He has been an inspiration to many who face difficult decisions in ministry. I am grateful for his example and for his friendship.

This book is also dedicated to Rev. Walter R. Jones and Rev. Sondra R. Jones, with thanksgiving for our enduring friendship. They are my dear friends, mentors, and shining examples of devotion to the Gospel of Jesus Christ.

Finally, this work is dedicated to David and Kathryn Melton, in the hope that we will always be together on the journey of faith.

ISBN 978-0-88177-560-0

Library of Congress Control Number 2009937749

This resource is published by Discipleship Resources in the hope that it will help congregations in planning. Discipleship Resources and the General Board of Discipleship are not engaged in legal, accounting, or other professional advising services. If legal advice or other expert assistance is required, the services of a professional advisor should be sought. This book does not establish a standard of care for local churches. Each local church makes its own decisions and determines what is best for it, and this book is intended only to provide information that may be helpful to some churches.

This resource contains hypothetical stories illustrating situations commonly occurring in ministry. All of the stories are hypothetical.

Table of Contents

Introduction

At the intersection of a minister's perception of the role of minister and a parishioner's perception of that role is the beginning of an interactive relationship in which trust and integrity are presupposed by all. Together, we believe, we will be able to live and work as disciples making the Gospel visible in the world. We, the ministers, enter into this relationship with confidence that having been called by God and ordained by the church, we will be working within a community of faith that is amenable to our leadership. The parishioners expect their ministers to be spiritual guides, Christian education teachers, financial analysts, construction project managers, preachers, friends, youth group leaders, relationship counselors, evangelists, and visitors of the sick.

Truth be told, it isn't often that the minister the congregants have called is fully aware of all their expectations or is capable of successfully meeting them. Here, then, is the beginning point of a relationship that can become strong and healthy for the parties or instead, can become contentious, conflicted, and lacking in harmony. *Safe Sanctuaries for Ministers* guides both ministers and parishioners to evaluate ethical questions and dilemmas of trust with the goal of acting in ways that will preserve the integrity of the ministry and extend the mission of the Church.

Joy T. Melton
jmelton@umcpact.org
770-512-8383

The Ministry of Christian Discipleship

On Palm Sunday of 1998, a twelve-year-old girl was kidnapped from her church just before she would have participated in the Palm processional with the Youth Choir. Providentially, the child survived the kidnapping and physical injuries and was quickly reunited with her family. The very next day, *Safe Sanctuaries: Reducing the Risk of Child Abuse* was published by Discipleship Resources. Since then, the United Methodist Church and other denominations have made determined efforts to stem the tide of child abuse in our ministries and communities of faith. Virtually every day has brought media reports of new and ever more horrifying incidents of abuse in churches of all descriptions. We have learned of congregations targeted as convenient places to find children who will be ritually sexually abused as sacrifices in a cult's rituals. We have learned of churches where the youth minister or athletic coaches use video cell phones and computers to film the members of the youth group or of the team and then turn those images into pornography displayed on the internet. We know of congregations where predators have obtained email addresses of members of the youth group and used that information to lure them into dangerous meetings that were meant to end in sexual abuse. We have learned that sexual predators are most often persons that are known and trusted by their victims, sometimes

Notes:

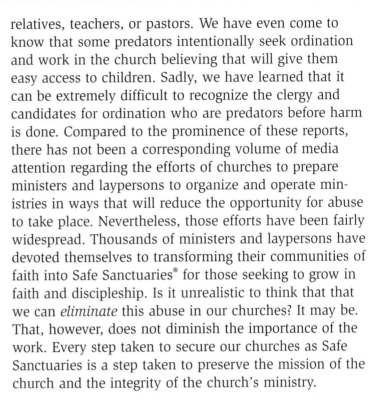

relatives, teachers, or pastors. We have even come to know that some predators intentionally seek ordination and work in the church believing that will give them easy access to children. Sadly, we have learned that it can be extremely difficult to recognize the clergy and candidates for ordination who are predators before harm is done. Compared to the prominence of these reports, there has not been a corresponding volume of media attention regarding the efforts of churches to prepare ministers and laypersons to organize and operate ministries in ways that will reduce the opportunity for abuse to take place. Nevertheless, those efforts have been fairly widespread. Thousands of ministers and laypersons have devoted themselves to transforming their communities of faith into Safe Sanctuaries® for those seeking to grow in faith and discipleship. Is it unrealistic to think that that we can *eliminate* this abuse in our churches? It may be. That, however, does not diminish the importance of the work. Every step taken to secure our churches as Safe Sanctuaries is a step taken to preserve the mission of the church and the integrity of the church's ministry.

Policies and procedures for best practices are particularly needed to reduce the incidence of clergy sexual misconduct. The sexual misconduct of clergy persons involving adults, rather than children, is reported almost as often as child abuse. The harm done in this type of case can be as devastating as in a case of child abuse. These cases often seem to start with the clergy person offering the parishioner, or the church employee, counseling or comfort in a time of stress. Sometimes these cases develop when the clergy person works closely with a parishioner on some church project and begins to try to introduce a sexual dimension into the relationship, thereby violating the sacred trust and covenant of the clergy—parishioner interaction. Regardless of how the clergy person describes the beginning of these cases, when the parishioner, or co-worker, describes the clergy person's behavior as unwanted, abusive, or uncomfortable, the result is that the integrity of the ministry is damaged, for the individual clergy person and also for all other ministers. Every time a clergy person engages in sexual misconduct, the trust level between clergy and parishioners is diminished. When the abusive clergy person leaves the congregation, the parishioners will be less inclined to trust that the new minister will act with integrity and honor.

Have you ever been the clergy person who follows a minister accused of sexual misconduct? It cannot be described as an easy job to do. By the time the new minister arrives, the congregation may have already experienced significant injury in several ways. The media may have saturated the community with unflattering coverage. Factions may have formed and divided the congregation between those who believe the victim's allegations and those who believe the minister's denials. Offerings and tithes may have declined. The nominations committee may find it very difficult to recruit members to serve in key leadership positions. There may be litigation pending and if so, there will be fewer resources available for ministry until the litigation ends. I once met a minister serving a church following this type of abuse. This minister was the fourteenth minister to serve the church since the abuse incident. None of the thirteen preceding ministers had been able to stay more than two years because the congregation was so devastated that they couldn't really function. Each new minister wound up depressed and exhausted in very short order. By the time this minister arrived, the church essentially had two separate congregations. One group believed the woman's allegations of abuse. The other group believed the accused pastor's denial. Each group's hostility toward the other was so deep that all the members of one group sat on one side of the sanctuary and the members of the other group sat on the other side. When the offering was taken each week, it was taken by two sets of ushers because neither group was willing to cross the aisle and

pass the offering plate to the other group. This shows just how crippled a congregation can be when its ministerial leaders have failed. Can we put a dollar value on the damage that is done to an individual victim, the congregation, or the mission of the whole church? The damage is incalculable.

My first experience of working with survivors of clergy sexual abuse was with adults who had been abused by their pastors. Their reports were more gruesome than I would have imagined possible. The depth of devastation the survivors described was matched only by the decibel level of the denials being made by the accused clergy perpetrators. It was true then, and still is, that many of the voices of denial were colleagues of the accused perpetrators. Their responses sounded like, "Oh, I know him and he would never do such a thing. He's happily married. Maybe she just misunderstood." Others responded, "Well it doesn't surprise me that she is telling such a tale. She flirts with every minister she meets. Everybody knows that." I always wonder why a colleague, who was never a witness to the interaction between the victim and the accused clergy person, would think that comments like these were appropriate. I don't have an answer; but I do know that in virtually every case an anthem of denial is raised on behalf of the accused perpetrator. This behavior does not serve to preserve the integrity of the mission and ministry of the church. It simply persuades the community members that clergy are less trustworthy than they would have hoped and expected. Sexual misconduct by clergy persons injures the church and destroys the Safe Sanctuary® every bit as much as child abuse.

This problem can readily be addressed by clergy leaders who are willing to engage in ministry based on the best professional ethical practices they can learn. First, we clergy persons must squelch our impulse to deny the reality of sexual abuse perpetrated by our fellow clergy.

Second, we must stop defending each other with attitudes minimizing or denying the issues and expressed like this: "I don't see what the big deal is. Lots of people commit adultery—ministers are no different." Third, we must claim for ourselves the truth that clergy persons are expected to be different—better able to control our self-centeredness and better able to put other's needs ahead of our own—all the time, even when we are out of the office or on vacation. Fourth, we must admit that we have, by our ordination, agreed to be different in these ways and model these behaviors in all that we do. Finally, by modeling best ethical practices we will transform our communities of faith into Safe Sanctuaries®. When we embody in our actions the true nature of the sacred trust between a minister and a parishioner we will be doing the work of the gospel.

Concurrently, alongside the reports of child abuse and clergy sexual misconduct, we have seen large numbers of reports of other catastrophic abuses in churches. Financial abuses are more frequent than we want to believe. Ministers and lay workers are caught with their pockets full of offerings that were meant to support the mission of the congregation. Ministers, trustees, and church treasurers fail in their duties by not conducting annual independent audits of the church's finances, and by not implementing internal controls with procedures for checks and balances to safeguard the church's resources and the individual members. The result is that funds disappear without a trace and the ministry and mission of the church is diminished by lack of resources. Members of personnel committees fail the church when hiring employees without checking personal references, conducting interviews, and processing criminal background checks. Learning that the recently hired business manager has a criminal record for theft and embezzlement after a large portion of the church's benevolent fund goes missing is learning too late. What will it take to restore the integrity of the mission of the church in

Notes:

Notes:

such a situation? What will it take to restore confidence in the trustworthiness of the minister's leadership in such a circumstance?

Almost always in risk management consultations with churches the question arises from the clergy: "What about us? How can Safe Sanctuaries® protect us? We are abused too and we deserve better." The frequency of these questions makes it clear that for a host of reasons, the ministers who are leading communities of faith today do not perceive themselves as either powerful role models or authority figures. Oddly enough, the parishioners of these ministers have a different perception. In the eyes of parishioners, the minister is a role model par excellence and a powerful authority figure. Parishioners hope to be guided, educated, and inspired by their ministers, no matter how the ministers perceive themselves or the parishioners. Perhaps it is this contradiction that underlies the loud cry of denial from clergy and the sob of disappointment and betrayal from parishioners when allegations of abuse and misconduct are made. It is certainly the feeling of disappointment and betrayal that sends parishioners, and others, into the machinations of criminal and civil litigation against clergy persons, churches, and denominations.

Safe Sanctuaries for Ministers can help.

This volume is intended as a helpful reference for those who have answered the holy call into the ordained ministry and for those who are members of churches, congregations, and communities of faith. Those who do the work of the ordained ministry do not simply have jobs, or careers, that can be attended to and accomplished within a predetermined amount of time each day or each week. Those who do the work of ordained ministry have accepted an invitation to "be" that is transformational. The invitation into ordained ministry is more than a simple job offer. The invitation calls us into a way of living and working that encompasses our whole lives, not just a single dimension of our work days. Recently, in a discussion of professional ethics for those in ministry, I heard one minister say, "When are we *not* ministers?" In other words, for those in some other types of work, there might be ethical codes applicable to the workplace but not to the other areas of their lives. However, for those of us in ministry, our ethical standards must pervade and enthuse every part of our lives.

The group discussion mentioned above was among medical doctors, lawyers, and clergy persons. The topics were: a comparison of the educational requirements for entering each profession and the practical "candidacy" requirements for each profession. Lawyers must complete a law school education, pass a certification examination (commonly referred to as the "bar exam"), pass a professional ethics examination, and pass an examination of their character and fitness for the profession before being licensed to practice law. Then, the usual practice is for the newly approved lawyer to work in a law firm as an "associate" for five to seven years, gaining hours and hours of valuable experience. The path into medical practice is very similar. First, the aspiring doctor completes education in medical school including internships; then, completes a period of "residency" that is several years long before completing a certification and character examination and being approved and licensed to practice medicine. To enter the ranks of ordained clergy, most denominations require completion of some level of theological education, although not all denominations require completion of graduate level degrees. Then, the candidate must work successfully in ministry for a period of several years before being finally approved for ordination. There is no requirement of completion of a standardized substantive certification examination; however, some denominations do require completion of several specific written papers on theological topics. There is no standardized written ethics examination included in the

Notes:

"WHEN ARE WE *NOT* MINISTERS?"

13

candidacy process for ordination; however, the candidate for ordination must usually successfully complete oral interviews in front of a committee of the Board of Ordained Ministry (in the United Methodist Church) or a similar group and these interviews may include questions related to professional ethics. In our group discussion, we arrived at a consensus that the candidacy and preparation requirements for each profession are similar in many ways. The lawyers and doctors were surprised by the lack of education and examination of professional ethics included in the ordination process for clergy. The question was asked, "Don't clergy want this kind of preparation? You are often more closely connected to persons making ultimate decisions than we are."

As the conversation continued, the doctors and lawyers also acknowledged, as the clergy had, that in reality we are doctors, lawyers, and clergy all the time, not just during regular work hours!

Responsibilities of the Laity

Those of us who are members of, and involved in, communities of faith as lay persons have responsibilities and obligations toward the community, too. Lay persons must participate faithfully and honestly by offerings of time, talent, service, and witness in furtherance of the mission and ministry of the congregation. These responsibilities include proper stewardship of the financial resources and supervision of the staff members of the congregation. These responsibilities include adequate maintenance of the church's property and physical plant.

There is enough work for everyone. I've never visited a community of faith that claimed to have more members than it needed to accomplish its mission and ministry. I've never met a minister who had more volunteers than jobs to be filled. On the other hand, I have worked with many churches where the members were loath to provide volunteer leadership and hesitant to take on any responsibility because there was misconduct on the part of the minister and trust in ministerial integrity had been destroyed.

Each time an incident of financial malfeasance by a clergy person or a lay employee is reported, in public media or on the "grapevine" that runs through the membership, the next stewardship campaign becomes more difficult. The results are decreased giving and diminished ministry. When our ministries are diminished in such a way, there is a domino effect that eventually leads to the demise of ministries. Financial malfeasance, whether it is outright intentional theft or simple negligence on the part of the clergy, devastates the integrity of the ordained ministry in the eyes of the congregation.

Notes:

LEADERSHIP IS TO BE
shared by clergy
and laity.

Scriptural Foundations for Setting Aside the Clergy

Both the Old and New Testaments provide accounts of the faith community identifying certain individuals for ordained leadership in matters of worship, mission, and evangelism. The stories of Aaron, Joshua, and Samuel are early records of individuals being called from the community into leadership roles for the community.

The Scriptures give us insights into more than five thousand years of the history of people of faith. We know the priests also fulfilled the roles of lawyer and judge in guiding the community. Aaron was not only the leader of worship; he was also an authority figure in the daily business of the people. Samuel served as a religious leader and had the responsibility for recognizing and anointing the king. By the time of the Roman occupation of Palestine, the separation of the faith community leadership and the secular community leadership had clearly been made. Religious leaders were not secular government authorities. The clergy were relied upon for teaching, leading worship, spiritual guidance in decision-making, and preserving the faith

Notes:

PREACH THE GOSPEL
always. Use words when necessary.

St. Francis

traditions. The second chapter of the Gospel of Luke provides us with examples of such expectations and how the clergy functioned to fulfill the expectations. The first part of the second chapter of Luke records the story of Mary and Joseph bringing the baby Jesus to the Temple for dedication. They relied on the priests to perform this traditional ritual and bless the child. Later in the second chapter of Luke, we are told about Jesus' trip to the Temple for celebrating Passover when he was twelve years old. When his parents begin to wonder where he is, they find him in conversation with the priests, the men who had been his teachers of faith. The Gospel of John illustrates that Jesus identified specific individuals for specific roles to spread the gospel. Peter was called to be the shepherd of the believers. John was called to be the witness—the reporter—of Jesus' ministry.

Today, in most Christian denominations, this identification and division of labor is still instituted. Parishioners rely on their ordained leaders to teach the values set out in the Christian gospel. Parishioners believe that the ordained leaders will not only teach through their words but also will live according to the same high standards and teach by example. St. Francis is believed to have taught, "Preach the Gospel always. Use words when necessary." In our society, St. Francis' approach to leadership remains as relevant for leadership as it must have been in his day. Every congregation is filled with parishioners hoping to have clergy leaders who provide leadership by example, not just by preaching in words.

When the faith community recognizes gifts for leadership in an individual and places that person into service as an ordained or commissioned minister, the community has high expectations. The minister's failure to lead with integrity and to model behavior adhering to the tenets of the communities' beliefs creates a crisis of faith at the very least. Today, such a crisis of faith may lead to criminal investigation and to litigation. When investigations begin, it is not unreasonable to expect that the congregation will be tied up in the crisis for years.

Notes:

Ordering Clergy Roles

As the community of faith grows, the needs of the people grow and become ever more complex. The need for clergy leadership capable of addressing many needs and issues encourages the community, clergy and lay, to develop ways to order their roles and organize their work. Each denomination has a systematic approach for accomplishing this. In my own denomination, the United Methodist Church, the ministry of the laity is recognized first. Then, we recognize several different roles for ordained ministry: local pastor, diaconal minister, elder, and deacon. Persons who believe they are called into any of these roles become candidates for ordination or commissioning. The candidacy process is long and complex. The goal is to adequately prepare each candidate with the education and skills that will be needed for service in ministry. Throughout the candidacy period candidates are involved in developing, or strengthening, their knowledge and their values so that upon their ordination, they are satisfactorily prepared to lead the community of faith. Hopefully, they are able to fulfill the high expectations of the parishioners.

The United Methodist denomination, as well as others, recognizes two ordained roles that are fairly similar. Deacons and elders are both authorized to preach. Deacons are especially expected to serve all people, particularly the poor, sick, and oppressed. Deacons interpret to the community of faith the needs of the world and demonstrate by their lives and teaching that serving the disadvantaged is serving Christ. Elders are expected to preach and also to administer the sacraments and preserve the order of the church.

CLERGY, AS SURELY AS doctors and lawyers, will face questions of professional ethics every day.

Notes:

On the occasion of ordination, deacon and elder candidates are examined and inquiry is made as to each candidate's willingness to live according to the example of Christ. Each candidate is expected to answer positively when asked if he or she will make a complete dedication of themselves to the ideals of the Christian gospel and demonstrate this dedication by the exercise of self-control, practice of personal habits that will support physical health, fidelity in marriage, celibacy in singleness, and integrity in every personal relationship. Each candidate does, in fact, answer these questions positively. This is a watershed moment in the life of each candidate. By making the choice to seek ordination, we choose to work on behalf of others and we acknowledge the trust placed in us to support the nurture of faith and discipleship in the congregation and the world. The Church has prepared each individual for ordained ministry and accepted each one. Now, the newly ordained minister must strive to fulfill the high standards of the community of faith.

The Ministry of the Clergy

Virtually every denomination has clearcut processes for identifying and training those individuals who will be clergy leaders in their communities of faith. In my denomination, there are specific requirements that each candidate for ordination must meet. There are educational requirements, work experience requirements, and character requirements that must be successfully completed before being approved for ordination.

The educational requirements in The United Methodist Church are extensive, including completion of courses such as Old Testament, New Testament, Church History, Church Polity and Administration, Systematic Theology, Worship, and Pastoral Counseling. Curiously, there are no requirements for any courses that would teach professional ethics for ministry. Law schools not only require courses in professional ethics for graduation, but passing an examination focused on professional ethics is also required before the student can be licensed to practice law. Medical schools provide courses in professional ethics and the ethical dilemmas the students will likely face in the practice of medicine.

Why, then, are such courses not provided for students seeking ordination? Surely, ordained ministers are just as likely as doctors or lawyers to face questions of ethics in their daily work. In fact, the ministers may face the need to guide a parishioner in ethical dilemmas, such as in making end-of-life health care decisions, before either the lawyer or the doctor is brought into the discussion. Why should the first professionals consulted, the ministers, be any less educated and prepared to guide their parishioners than the doctor is prepared to advise her patients? I have posed this question to seminary professors, academic deans, Board of Ministry members, and a bishop or two. Let me summarize their answers: "We have so many academic requirements for graduation, and additional academic requirements for ordination, that there is simply no more room in the curriculum. Besides, all the candidates for ordination were raised from childhood in the Christian faith, so they already know how to act ethically in the ministry. "

My colleagues would not intend their answers to be perceived as short-sighted or naive. But it occurs to me that if the other professions, medicine and law, make this type of education a priority, the church really must, too. Law schools and medical schools do not make the unrealistic assumption that their students were "raised from childhood" in any way that would guarantee their ability to make appropriate ethical decisions. Perhaps a generation or two ago, it would have been reasonable to assume that the candidates for ordination were raised from childhood in the Christian faith. Today, that assumption is not valid. Some individuals who are

Notes:

seeking ordination had no experience with Christian faith until they were adults. Their ethical decision-making ability was formed outside a community of faith and may or may not conform to Christian values. Some individuals seek ordination because after failing in their first or second careers, they are looking for work that will guarantee them a home, a retirement fund, and employment, no matter how effective their work will be. These persons may, or may not have ethical values and priorities drawn from their commitment to the Christian faith. Their values may be drawn from their experiences in their previous workplaces, or from their previous occupational peer group, rather than from a community of faith. Relying on such persons' experience to adequately equip them to make appropriate decisions and choose ethical behaviors in every situation is risky, at best. At worst, this kind of assumption leads to the ordination or commissioning of persons who may very well have inadequate education and foundations for providing ethical leadership in the community of faith.

The evidence of this risk is to be found in the rising tide of litigation against churches for the misconduct of their clergy leaders. It seems logical that if the Church had better educated its clergy for appropriate decision making, and brought consequences to bear in instances of bad decision making or unethical behavior, then the current litigation crisis might have been averted, at least in some measure. From my perspective, as a clergy person and attorney who represents churches in litigation, preventing suits through sound preparation for ministry, and continuing training in ministry would go a long way toward preserving the monetary resources of the church and would also help to preserve the integrity of the ordained ministry in the perception of parishioners and the public.

We don't have any figures for how much it would cost to implement systematic professional ethics education for those who seek ordination or commissioning. However, the costs of litigation against churches have been well documented. The Roman Catholic Church in America has admitted that such litigation has cost nearly a billion dollars. Recently, one diocese held an auction of its real property in hopes of raising enough money to pay litigation expenses. Another diocese has declared bankruptcy. The public declaration of bankruptcy refers to financial bankruptcy; but, at the level of spiritual leadership in the minds of parishioners, it demonstrates the spiritual bankruptcy of the clergy leaders.

Other Christian churches can report litigation costs in the multi-million dollar range. This problem is certainly not limited to the Roman Catholic Church, or any other single denomination. In the past three years, cases in several protestant denominations have been settled, or taken to trial, resulting in multi-million dollar losses for the churches and denominations. Since 2001, the National Committee for the Prevention of Child Abuse has shown that the annual costs of child abuse in the United States exceed one hundred billion dollars, not including the costs of litigation against churches. Child abuse is not the only reason churches are being drawn into litigation. Thus, the costs are actually even higher than any of the figures shared here.

What would be the best practice, from a perspective of developing skills for professional ethical decision making by clergy persons, for the Church as it examines the education requirements for those seeking ordination and a place in professional ministry as well as for those already ordained? Academic courses are one practice; but, other practices are needed throughout the length of each person's ministry. Every clergy person will have an individual answer to this question. The most obvious practice is a planned program of continuing education courses focused on the substance and content of appropriate ethical practices for ministry. My own vision would be a

Notes:

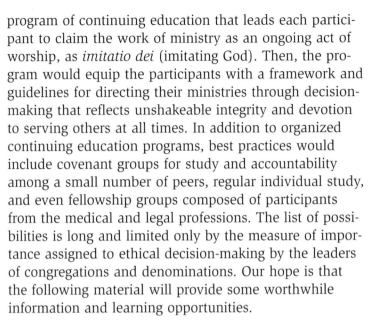

program of continuing education that leads each partici-pant to claim the work of ministry as an ongoing act of worship, as *imitatio dei* (imitating God). Then, the pro-gram would equip the participants with a framework and guidelines for directing their ministries through decision-making that reflects unshakeable integrity and devotion to serving others at all times. In addition to organized continuing education programs, best practices would include covenant groups for study and accountability among a small number of peers, regular individual study, and even fellowship groups composed of participants from the medical and legal professions. The list of possi-bilities is long and limited only by the measure of impor-tance assigned to ethical decision-making by the leaders of congregations and denominations. Our hope is that the following material will provide some worthwhile information and learning opportunities.

Educational preparation for ordination is only one facet of the candidacy process. In The United Methodist Church, as well as others, another crucial part of the process is a series of personal interviews between the candidate and several groups of persons. These interviews are conduct-ed at several specific times during the candidacy process. The candidate is interviewed by members of his or her local church, then by members of the district board of ministry, then by members of the annual conference board of ministry. All of the interviewing groups must conclude that the candidate meets the standards for ordi-nation, or approval for ordination is not granted.

This interview process is very detailed but also very sub-jective and certainly unpredictable. Nevertheless, this part of the process is absolutely essential. Sexual preda-tors are often skillful liars in conversation and even in formal interviews. That doesn't mean that conducting personal interviews is a waste of time. It simply means that interviews must not be relied on as the sole basis for deciding to approve a candidate's ordination.

Imagine this as an example of what a persuasive liar a predator can be: A man entered the ordination candidacy process telling everyone who interviewed him that he felt called by God to go into a chaplaincy ministry with incarcerated juvenile offenders. He believed these were the least, the lost, and the loneliest individuals in society and that he could bring the gospel to them. Every group he interviewed with was enthralled by his charismatic persona and his enthusiasm for the vision of ministry he expressed. He was approved and ordained. Before long, several of the offenders he was supposed to serve as chaplain reported that he was sexually abusing them. The result of the investigation of their complaints was that he plead guilty to multiple criminal charges and was sentenced to a lengthy prison term. This example does not teach us that interviews are not useful. It teaches us that interviews with potential clergy persons must be combined with other tools for evaluating the candidate's gifts and graces for ministry, such as attentive supervision of the individual's work.

The ordination candidacy process begins when an individual approaches his or her local church and seeks the church's support and approval for ordination. Therefore, the local church members must have a clear understanding of the roles and responsibilities of lay persons and clergy persons. They also need to be able to discern the applicant's talents for serving as lay or clergy. Providing regular preparation for the local committees could help reduce the risk of eventual clergy misconduct. By providing such assistance, we can give local committees greater power to decline to support the candidacy of doubtfully qualified applicants.

Yet another dimension of the candidacy process is successful work in ministry settings over a period of time. Every member of a church's personnel committee understands from personal work experiences in the secular world, the importance of a strong supervision and

Notes:

ATTENTIVE SUPERVISION
of new clergy will lead to development of ethical best practices.

evaluation process for new members of the staff. The supervision and evaluation processes must be intentional and attentive in order to be useful and constructive. In my work with churches, too often I find that the opportunities for supervision and correction of a now-accused staff member were squandered. For example, instead of counseling the youth minister regarding appropriate uses of email and other technology before a problem arises, no guidance is provided. Then, a problem comes along, and the supervisor's only response is, "I assumed he knew better than that." A lawyer defending a church in litigation always dreads those words, "I assumed. . .". Assumptions like these lead to costly consequences, if not in litigation, then certainly in the loss of trust from the parishioners.

There is another value of attentive supervision. Sexual predators seek out work opportunities that will afford easy and quick access to children or youth with as little supervision as possible. Congregations are seen as easy targets because there are plenty of children and few, if any, staff members giving attentive supervision. Understanding these realities can and should lead a congregation to take a more active approach to the supervision and ongoing evaluation of all its staff members, both clergy and lay, paid and volunteer. Congregations where the supervision principles of Safe Sanctuaries® are followed routinely reduce the likelihood that predators can be successful.

This brief review of the general parameters of the ordination process is offered to highlight the points at which members of the local congregation have responsibilities and obligations. By fulfilling all of these responsibilities, we can help prevent the ordination of persons who are not appropriate candidates and reduce the possible losses associated with clergy misconduct.

Financial Standards in Professional Ministry

chapter three

Stewardship of our Resources for Ministry

One of the most crucial responsibilities for ministers is the steward-ship of the church's resources for ministry. Beyond leading an annual fundraising campaign in a local congregation, this responsibility includes many facets. There is no need for any fundraising campaign unless the congregation has formed a vision of ministry the members believe they want to engage in, or should engage in. Creating a vision for ministry will certainly involve consideration of all of the church's resources and how best to utilize them: funds on hand, available facilities, persons and their skills or talents, and many other resources. Those who will be participants in the ministry will also need to take stock of their personal resources including their health, enthusiasm, and time availability.

What qualifications are most needed in the clergy who lead the con-gregation in the stewardship of resources for the mission and min-

Notes:

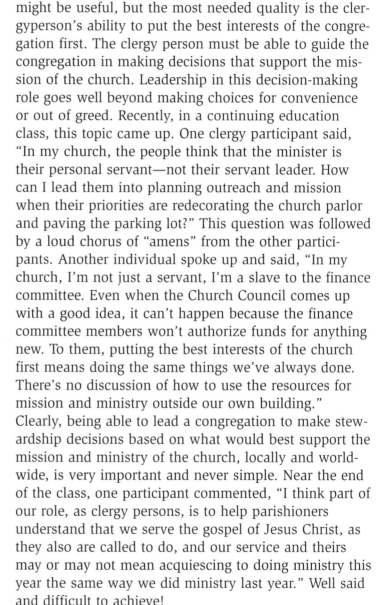

istry of the church? Should the list include qualities such as salesmanship, friendliness, competitiveness, or a college degree in finance and accounting? Any of these might be useful, but the most needed quality is the clergyperson's ability to put the best interests of the congregation first. The clergy person must be able to guide the congregation in making decisions that support the mission of the church. Leadership in this decision-making role goes well beyond making choices for convenience or out of greed. Recently, in a continuing education class, this topic came up. One clergy participant said, "In my church, the people think that the minister is their personal servant—not their servant leader. How can I lead them into planning outreach and mission when their priorities are redecorating the church parlor and paving the parking lot?" This question was followed by a loud chorus of "amens" from the other participants. Another individual spoke up and said, "In my church, I'm not just a servant, I'm a slave to the finance committee. Even when the Church Council comes up with a good idea, it can't happen because the finance committee members won't authorize funds for anything new. To them, putting the best interests of the church first means doing the same things we've always done. There's no discussion of how to use the resources for mission and ministry outside our own building." Clearly, being able to lead a congregation to make stewardship decisions based on what would best support the mission and ministry of the church, locally and worldwide, is very important and never simple. Near the end of the class, one participant commented, "I think part of our role, as clergy persons, is to help parishioners understand that we serve the gospel of Jesus Christ, as they also are called to do, and our service and theirs may or may not mean acquiescing to doing ministry this year the same way we did ministry last year." Well said and difficult to achieve!

The Book of Discipline's Standards

The Book of Discipline sets forth, for United Methodist churches, the standards by which the resources of the churches are to be cared for. Every denomination has a resource similar to *The Book of Discipline* that is used to articulate the standards for the stewardship of the churches' resources. The standards are meant to safeguard the resources of a congregation from waste, from inappropriate uses, and from theft. Generally, these standards include the following at a minimum:

1. A finance committee composed of members of the congregation.
2. A church treasurer who will disburse all funds to the appropriate causes that are included in the church's budget and who will make regular financial reports to the finance committee and church council.
3. The treasurer and financial secretary shall be bonded.
4. A financial secretary who is not in the immediate family of the church treasurer.
5. Offerings should be counted by two persons who are not in the same immediate family.
6. The financial secretary shall receive a report of the offering and shall keep records of all contributions and all payments.
7. An annual independent audit of the records of the church's financial officers and the church's organizations shall be authorized by the finance committee and the report submitted to the church council, or other appropriate body.
8. A board of trustees composed of church members.
9. The trustees shall be responsible for the supervision and care of all the church's real and personal property. The trustees shall also be responsible for acquiring adequate liability insurance for the church property and personnel.
10. The trustees shall administer all bequests, trusts, and other such funds received by the church.

Notes:

29

10. The trustees shall administer all bequests, trusts, and other such funds received by the church.

This list is not exhaustive. Guidelines like these are meant to be thorough but each congregation needs to set its policies and procedures in light of its specific ministries. They are effective because they create a system of checks and balances in the handling of the church's resources and meeting the church's obligations. However, without persistent vigilance and adherence to these standards, abuses could occur with costly consequences for the church. Furthermore, these guidelines do not give the minister of the congregation, or any members of the minister's family, any authority with regard to financial accounts.

Hypothetical Cases

Let's look at a few examples of situations your church could face. These examples are hypothetical and designed for your study purposes only.

Hypothetical Case No. 1

Assume the following details. First Church was fairly small fifteen years ago. A new pastor was called and before long, there seemed to be a growing sense of well-being and enthusiasm among the parishioners. Giving and tithing began to go up substantially. After three years of steady growth, the financial secretary and the church treasurer, who were both parishioners and served as volunteers in their positions, suggested to the pastor that it would be good to hire a full-time church business manager. The pastor, finance committee, and trustees considered the idea and agreed. Coincidentally, a member of the board of trustees had an adult son who was looking for a job. He told his son about the job opening.

The son sent an application and a resume to the church's personnel committee and asked for an interview. Following a cursory meeting with the committee members in which they expressed their happiness that this young man had returned to his "home church," he was hired for the business manager's position. Although the young man provided several personal and employment references, none of them was contacted by the committee.

The church continued to grow, in membership, over the next eight years. However, the financial growth of the church gradually slowed down. The finance committee and the church council regularly reviewed the business manager's reports of contributions and expenditures, but neither the finance committee nor the pastor ever called for an audit.

In the business manager's ninth year of employment, the pastor retired and the church called a new pastor. Within a few weeks of her arrival, the new pastor asked to see the annual reports of the financial audit for the past three years. She was astonished to find that no audits had been conducted for the past fifteen years. Immediately, an independent audit was arranged. The audit clearly showed why the financial growth of the church had begun to slow down after the business manager was hired. The plate offering amounts dwindled quickly from approximately ten percent of weekly contributions to only one or two percent. Additionally, some trust funds were depleted for questionable reasons. Finally, a larger and larger amount of church funds was devoted to expense reimbursements for the business manager and the former pastor. The auditors concluded that several hundred thousand dollars had vanished.

The ensuing investigation revealed that the business manager had systematically siphoned off large amounts

Notes:

of cash from the weekly plate offerings and had reimbursed himself for imaginary expenses. He had also managed to convince the trustees that the church's trust fund really only needed one person to sign checks and that he would gladly handle this chore. Eventually the business manager was charged with numerous crimes related to theft and fraud and received a lengthy prison sentence. The minister is still enjoying retirement.

What guidelines and procedures could First Church have used to prevent such losses? What would you recommend to your own church, and your clergy colleagues, as the best ethical practices for good stewardship of the church's resources?

In the beginning, the church leaders and the pastor were doing well by sharing information, by having two persons (treasurer and financial secretary) involved in making deposits and expenditures, by having several persons count each week's offerings, and by regularly reviewing the financial reports and all accounts of the church. When the decision was made to recruit a business manager, the pastor and members of the finance committee included the personnel committee members in the decision-making. The personnel committee interviewed only one applicant, the trustee's son.

Things began to go wrong at this point. The personnel committee did well by collecting a written application for the position from the applicant. However, they failed to thoroughly review the information on the application and the resume. The pastor did not review the resume or participate in the interview. They did not ask the candidate why he had returned to their community after living out west for several years. They asked nothing about his previous work experience. They didn't check with any of the references he listed on the application.

If any of the references had been contacted, they might have revealed that they had no knowledge of the applicant's suitability for the job because they had not been in contact with him for many years. This could have alerted the committee members to ask for additional, and more up-to-date, references. It should also have alerted the committee to follow through with contacting the additional references. If the committee had simply taken this step, the church might have been spared a terrible tragedy.

The application did not ask the applicant to consent to having a criminal background check conducted. It did not ask if the applicant had ever been convicted of any misdemeanor or felony criminal offenses. If the application had asked for consent to conduct the criminal background check, and the committee had actually had such a report completed, it could have revealed that the applicant had been convicted of theft, embezzlement, and fraud and had served a lengthy prison term. In other words, if the committee had checked the up-to-date references and completed a criminal background check on the applicant for all the addresses he had in the previous five to seven years, the church could have been spared the losses that followed the hiring of this man.

What would the costs to the committee and the congregation have been for using these two procedures? There would have been a time factor. Some members of the committee would have given their time to interview the individuals named as references and to follow up with the applicant for additional references. The value of the committee members' time in conducting these interviews should not be minimized; however, as members of the congregation this is a contribution they are glad to make for the good of the church.

Processing a criminal background check, with the applicant's consent, would have involved the cost of paying

Notes:

for the records to be checked. Today, the usual fees for this type of background check ranges from ten dollars to thirty-five dollars. The results of the records check can be returned to the committee almost immediately, and certainly in a few days. Therefore, if this congregation had simply taken the time to check references and to process a criminal records check on the applicant, they might have "spent" thirty-five dollars and a few hours of time and achieved a result that would have protected the church from serious losses. A completed criminal background report should be a requirement for every applicant and no exceptions should be made to this policy.

After the new business manager was hired, the pastor and financial leaders still could have minimized the damage done by the business manager. First and foremost, the finance committee and pastor should have arranged for an independent audit every year. The likely result would have been one of two things: the business manager would not have dared to steal, knowing that his work was being reviewed and monitored, or his abuses would have been discovered much sooner and the losses thereby reduced. Furthermore, the financial secretary and treasurer could have been more attentive to the requests for expense reimbursement they received from the business manager and pastor. They should have required actual receipts for the expenses, not just handwritten notes. This procedure is so simple and straightforward that it almost seems silly to articulate it here. However, it is amazing how often cases of expense reimbursement abuses are reported. Pastors report that their predecessor abused the expense reimbursement policy of the congregation and now they are being unfairly restricted and scrutinized. This attitude reflects a failure of leadership and integrity on the part of the current pastor. Rather than complaining about adhering to such policies, the clergy leader must be the one to uphold and support these policies to demonstrate good stewardship of the congregation's resources.

The trustees and the pastor could have acted more responsibly by not entertaining the business manager's offer to act as the sole signatory on the church's trust funds.

The best ethical practices for preventing this type of situation, or reducing the losses in this situation, would include the basic guidelines listed at the beginning of this chapter. The best practices would also include:

- Making a criminal background check a requirement for any applicant;
- Checking all references given by the applicant; and
- Requiring a minimum of two signatures on each account, at least one of which is the church treasurer's and neither of which is the pastor's.

The costs to the congregation of following these best practices will always be minimal in comparison to the costs that will mount up as a result of the church's failure to follow the best practices.

The minister in a congregation like this one is often tempted to leave the oversight of financial matters solely to the members. When everything seems to be going smoothly, the minister rationalizes his or her minimal involvement with the thought that the church members know what they are doing and are honest people who don't need supervision. When everything isn't going smoothly, the minister rationalizes that his or her leadership wouldn't be enough to stop any abuses and would only make parishioners angry. Today, clergy leaders cannot afford to take either of these attitudes. Good stewardship of the resources of the community of faith is crucial to the mission and ministry of the church. The clergy are called to strong and cooperative leadership of the congregation in this area.

Notes:

BEST PRACTICES FOR recruiting and screening will reduce the likelihood of abuse.

Hypothetical Case No. 2

Assume the following details. This story is also from First Church. Assume the same facts as given in Hypothetical Case No. 1. The new pastor was, understandably, worried about the general state of the church's finances after the audit was completed. She, along with the Church Treasurer, Financial Secretary, and members of the finance committee, began a comprehensive review of every aspect of the church's accounts. It wasn't long before they discovered that the former business manager had failed to renew the incorporation of the church two years earlier, leaving them in an unincorporated status. Then they discovered that the business manager had not paid the premiums for the church's property and liability insurance for at least two years and the insurance had been canceled. The church trustees went to work immediately to reinstate the property and liability insurance and to re-establish the church's status as an incorporated non-profit organization.

Just when the pastor began to feel as if things were settling down, the chairman of the trustees came to show her the lawsuit he had been served with. The lawsuit named the church, the pastor, and all the individual trustees as defendants. The lawsuit alleged that a child had been injured on the church playground nearly one year ago because the playground equipment had not been properly maintained. The lawsuit sought to have the church pay the child's medical expenses and another additional amount to represent compensation for her pain and suffering.

If you have ever lived through a lawsuit involving your church, you know how difficult it can be. For First Church, it became even worse very quickly. The church's attorney informed them that there was no insurance coverage for the claim or for defense costs because the injury had happened after the former business manager let the insurance lapse and before the new insurance took effect. The litigation is still ongoing. The plaintiffs (the injured child and her parents) are reluctant to settle too quickly. They are angry not only because their child was injured but also because the former business manager had never responded to their first letter or to any of their phone calls. They have suffered and now they want the church to suffer too. Thus, within the new pastor's first six months at the church, First Church has suffered a substantial financial loss due to the theft perpetrated by the former business manager. First Church will also face additional financial losses as the lawsuit is processed. This is a situation that will influence First Church for the foreseeable future.

What are the best ethical practices that would have prevented this crisis if the new pastor or the church leaders had used them?

The pastor's best practices would have been:

1.

2.

3.

4.

The church leaders' best practices would have been:

1.

2.

3.

4.

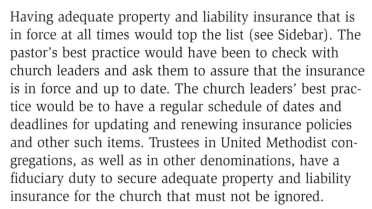

Notes:

Having adequate property and liability insurance that is in force at all times would top the list (see Sidebar). The pastor's best practice would have been to check with church leaders and ask them to assure that the insurance is in force and up to date. The church leaders' best practice would be to have a regular schedule of dates and deadlines for updating and renewing insurance policies and other such items. Trustees in United Methodist congregations, as well as in other denominations, have a fiduciary duty to secure adequate property and liability insurance for the church that must not be ignored.

Keeping the incorporation status up to date is a best practice because incorporation as a non-profit corporation can help to limit the liability of individual church members in the event of a lawsuit. The pastor's best practice would have been to check with church leaders about the incorporation status on an annual basis just as she checks with them about the insurance coverage. Similarly, the church leaders' best practice would be to include updating and renewing the incorporation of the church in the regular schedule of dates and other deadlines. For United Methodist churches, the status of incorporation, insurance coverages, and maintenance of the church property is to be included in the report of the Trustees at the annual Charge Conference. Records of the church's insurance coverages, incorporation, deeds to property, and other important documents need to be kept in the church's safe and they should also be maintained in the computer files of the church.

The pastor and the trustees should work together to plan how to respond to complaints such as a child's playground injury and the employees of the church should be well informed of the church's plan. The pastor must take the initiative to see that this is done before any complaint arises. The trustees must make regular safety inspections of church property and equipment a priority responsibility. If any repairs or improvements are

Insurance: How to Get It and Keep It

Stewardship of our churches' resources for ministry includes securing adequate property, personnel, and liability insurance for our congregations. Clergy leadership in cooperation with lay leadership in this facet of stewardship is crucial. In the interest of full disclosure, let me say that I serve as the Chief Resource Officer of the United Methodist Property and Casualty Trust, the captive, non-profit reinsurance company of the United Methodist Church. Every day I am involved with congregations across our denomination working to resource their ministries, including adequate insurance. For United Methodist churches and annual conferences, getting adequate insurance for the full spectrum of your ministries and your property is simply a matter of becoming an insured member of the United Methodist Property and Casualty Trust. For churches of other denominations, getting adequate insurance is a matter of purchasing coverage from a commercial insurance company in your community.

Traditionally, congregations have perhaps felt little urgency about securing adequate property and liability insurance for churches and their property. When anything happened to the buildings, the congregation would all get together and repair or rebuild to meet the needs. In today's world that isn't as easy as it sounds. Insurance for the replacement value of our properties is a best practice for stewardship that must not be ignored by the church trustees. Liability insurance, including coverage for directors and officers, clergy misconduct, and for employment practices, is also a best practice for stewardship because the frequency of litigation against churches for these types of claims has increased exponentially in recent years. Congregations who take a short-sighted view, saying "We don't need this insurance because we are a small church and no one would ever make a claim or file a lawsuit against us," are more and more frequently regretting such attitudes. When the congregation is named in a lawsuit, it is too late to secure insurance coverage for the allegations contained in that suit! Our current economic climate is difficult. Church leaders are working to stretch limited funds to keep ministry functioning. In times like these, insurance becomes more necessary and more beneficial than we have previously realized. In fact, one of the most successful church insurance companies in existence today was launched in the depths of the Great Depression.

Acquiring adequate and maintaining adequate insurance is a best practice of stewardship. The trustees of the congregation must review insurance coverages annually as well as inspect the property for maintenance and safety problems. They must then take action for corrective maintenance and for increasing or modifying coverage as needed.

needed, then the trustees must work to see that the repairs are completed. Above all, the pastor, finance committee, trustees, financial secretary, and church treasurer must actively maintain a strong system of checks and balances that will prevent the concentration of too much authority, or access to funds, in one person.

Hypothetical Case No. 3

Assume the following details. This hypothetical case comes from New Church. The name of the church refers to the new building the congregation moved into recently. The church was actually chartered more than thirty years ago. All of the charter members pitched in to get the church up and running. It didn't take them long to get comfortable with their volunteer roles. Some were Sunday School teachers, choir members, and nursery keepers. Others volunteered to be the Financial Secretary, Church Treasurer, and the members of the finance committee and board of trustees. By the time the congregation moved into the new building, the Financial Secretary and Church Treasurer had been serving in those positions since the church began.

New Church has a full-time pastor and a part-time choir director. There are no other staff members. The trustees and the pastor together decided on the items of office furniture and equipment that would be needed in the new building. At least, that is what the trustees thought they had done. Soon after the new building opened, a very large and very expensive copy/fax/scan machine was delivered. This machine looked like it could do everything except cook dinner. The pastor not only signed the delivery receipt, his was the sole signature on the lease contract. When the invoice arrived for the first lease payment, the Church Treasurer was caught by surprise. She asked the pastor if such a large payment amount could possibly be right. The pastor told her the amount was correct and there was nothing to worry about. But the Church Treasurer did worry. She knew the budget was tight and she didn't remember the trustees authorizing such an extravagant purchase.

Before the next meeting of the board of trustees, the pastor announced his retirement and moved away. The congregation began a search for a new pastor. During the next few months, attendance and giving declined. Finally, the Church Treasurer felt she had to consult the trustees about making the huge lease payments for the copy machine. The trustees were angry that the pastor had signed a lease contract without their knowledge. They authorized the Church Treasurer to contact the company from which the machine had been leased and ask that the church be allowed to return the machine. The company sent a truck to pick up the machine and they sent a notice to the church demanding payment in full of the remaining balance due on the lease contract. A series of phone calls between the lease company and the trustees took place. The trustees were unable to convince the lease company to reduce, or forgive, the balance due. The result was that the lease company filed a lawsuit against the church to collect the amount due.

What best practices could the pastor and the church leaders have used to prevent this kind of situation?

The pastor would have done well to use these practices:

1.

2.

3.

4.

Notes:

STRONG ETHICAL CLERGY
leadership recognizes the authority of lay members in matters of stewardship.

The church leaders would have done well to use these practices:

1.

2.

3.

4.

The first two hypotheticals shared illustrate how valuable it is for a church to have strong ethical leadership from the clergy. This story illustrates how detrimental it is for a church when the clergy take too much authority for financial matters and stewardship of the resources for ministry. The clergyperson needs to be knowledgeable about the congregation's financial matters and needs to be a role model for ethical decision-making. It is not unusual for the clergy leader of a congregation to be inexperienced in leadership related to financial issues. Thus, a mark of excellence in leadership would be to seek advice and guidance from knowledgeable and experienced persons, in the congregation or community. The clergyperson is not the chief executive officer of the congregation and must not have decision-making authority regarding expenditure of church funds.

The clergyperson is not the appropriate leader to enter into business relationships or contracts that obligate the congregation to a financial obligation. Thus, for the pastor and the trustees in this situation, the best practices would have included having the lease contract reviewed by the trustees, and if approved, then signed by the trustees. For most of its existence, New Church had successfully managed its financial resources and obligations by using a system of checks and balances that assured decisions were made by several persons, not a single individual. The congregation had become accustomed to working cooperatively with the pastor to make financial decisions. This had been their practice since the congregation was founded. When this pastor made a unilateral decision with very expensive consequences, the members were caught unaware.

Let's look at one more sample hypothetical case and analyze the ethical and stewardship issues it presents for the minister and for the congregation.

Hypothetical Case No. 4

Assume the following details. Friendship Church is a large congregation. Rev. Dogood, the pastor, has led the congregation for ten years and has become well liked and highly respected. He has earned a reputation for being an engaging preacher, an effective counselor, and a comforting visitor to the sick. He is also known as a good mentor for the younger and less experienced ministers on the clergy staff at the church.

Friendship Church's doctrine calls for its ministers and its members to abstain from the use of alcohol, tobacco, and any illegal substances. No one has ever seen Rev. Dogood drink any alcoholic beverage. He has openly preached against such practice. However, over the past couple of years, a few parishioners have noticed that he has put on a substantial amount of weight and his complexion has become red and blotchy. At times, he appears to be forgetful or confused about dates and appointments. When anyone mentions his weight gain to him, he replies, "Oh, you know it's just that curse of middle-age spread. My dad was the same way." If he forgets an appointment, or arrives late to a committee meeting, he brushes it off by saying he had too many things scheduled for the same time.

One day, the church secretary enters Rev. Dogood's office to deliver his daily mail. He is seated at his desk but he

appears to be sound asleep. As she comes nearer to the desk, she notices that the bottom drawer of his desk is open and it contains a nearly empty bottle of whiskey. The secretary quietly leaves his office. Later, she rings his phone extension to let him know there is someone waiting to see him. At the end of the workday, she leaves the church without letting the pastor know what she observed.

Soon after, Rev. Dogood is on the way to visit a new church member when he has a wreck in his car. The policeman at the scene reports that Rev. Dogood appears to have fallen asleep at the wheel and run off the road and down an embankment. Fortunately, no other vehicles were involved and no one was injured.

Last week, the chairman of the church's council came to see Rev. Dogood to plan for the next council meeting. He found Rev. Dogood in his office where he had passed out. His head was bleeding, apparently from hitting the corner of his desk as he fell to the floor. There was an empty liquor bottle on his desk. The church member called for an ambulance and followed it to the hospital. The next day several church members from the personnel committee came to the hospital to see the pastor. He admitted that he had a "drinking problem" and asked them to grant him some time off for the purpose of going into a therapeutic recovery program. Anxious to help in any way they could, they approved his request and assured him that the church would pay all the costs of the program.

Rev. Dogood went directly from the hospital to the recovery facility. In less than two weeks, he checked himself out of the program. He declared that he was "well enough" and would not drink any more. He also demanded a refund of half the fees the church had already paid on his behalf. The facility administrator provided the refund of several thousand dollars and then,

Rev. Dogood left the facility against the advice of the administrator.

The next morning, Rev. Dogood went to the church and told everyone that he had recovered more quickly than expected and was ready to get back to work. He didn't tell the church treasurer that the recovery facility had refunded the church's money directly to him. The members of the staff welcomed him back. It was only a matter of days before it became clear that Rev. Dogood hadn't really fully recovered. Early one evening, some of the members of the personnel committee arrived at the church for a meeting. Rev. Dogood's car was already parked in the church parking lot. When the church members reached the church office door, they found Rev. Dogood just inside and unconscious. The odor of alcohol was strong.

What actions must the personnel committee members take to act in the best interest of the church's stewardship of its resources for ministry? What actions must the minister take to act in the best interest of the church's ministry?

Use this space to make your list of actions that the congregation should or could take to preserve its resources for ministry:

1.

2.

3.

4.

Notes:

Use this space to make your list of actions that the minister could or should take to preserve the resources of the church and the integrity of the church's ministry in the larger community:

1.

2.

3.

4.

Let's begin with the minister. As the clergy leader of this congregation, Rev. Dogood must take action that will preserve the integrity of the ministry and reputation of the church in the whole community. Such action could include resigning as the pastor to clear the way for the congregation to call a new leader. This would, of course, be the most expedient action to take from the congregation's perspective. However, it would also probably be the most difficult to take from the minister's perspective. The congregation would be spared, to the extent possible, the negative publicity attached to situations like this. Furthermore, the pastor's resignation would spare the congregation any continuing financial responsibility or expenses for the pastor's problems. From the perspective of the pastor, outright resignation may lead to consequences for himself and his family that he is too afraid to encounter. Such consequences would very possibly include loss of income, loss of health and medical insurance, loss of a place to live, loss of a car, and probably more. In this situation, which set of consequences must we, as clergy persons, be most attentive to?

The pastor could take a leave of absence and use that time to seriously approach his recovery and rehabilitation from substance abuse. When the rehabilitation process is deemed to be successful, then it could be appropriate to seek reentry into active ministry. In the event Rev. Dogood does seek reentry into professional ministry, he will need to be truthful about his history of substance abuse and how he was affected. If his former church is contacted to give a recommendation or reference for him, then they too must be truthful about his history and how it affected the performance of his duties.

It would certainly be appropriate for the pastor to return the funds he collected from the rehabilitation facility. The church paid for his rehabilitation program in good faith that he would use this opportunity to fully recover. He did not complete the program and if any funds should have been returned, the church treasurer would have been the rightful recipient on behalf of the congregation.

What About the Best Practices for Preserving Clergy Resources?

These hypotheticals have focused on ethical violations perpetrated by clergy or church staff members resulting in harm to the church and its resources. Ministers must learn to guide their congregations in ethical decision-making regarding the use of church resources. Ministers must also learn to make ethical decisions regarding the use of their individual resources of time, health, even finances.

To illustrate, let's go back to Hypothetical No. 4 and assume these additional details: Rev. Dogood is married

Notes:

Notes:

BEST PRACTICES FOR stewardship of our physical health will also support the strength of our work.

to his college sweetheart. She is a school teacher and is working on a graduate degree at a nearby college in the evenings. Although she has taken out student loans to pay for tuition, she believes the debt will be offset by the better paying position she'll have after graduation. They don't have any children. The demands of her work and school schedule are heavy. She seldom gets home before midnight on the nights she attends class. By the time she arrives, Rev. Dogood is usually asleep. The mornings are rushed with no time for breakfast. Neither one of them engages in any kind of regular physical fitness activities. Both of them have gained some weight in the past few months. On Saturdays, she studies and does the housework. He polishes his sermon and visits parishioners who are in the hospital. Sundays are taken up with Sunday School and worship services. They haven't gone to a movie together, much less taken a vacation, since she started graduate school! He used to play golf occasionally; but, now he only reads Golf Digest.

Mrs. Dogood claims she had no idea that Rev. Dogood was drinking until the church members found him passed out at the church. She believes his brief visit in the rehabilitation clinic will solve this problem. All she wants is for them to be able to "get back to normal".

Use this space to make a list of actions that the minister could take to strengthen his physical health:

1.

2.

3.

Use this space to make a list of actions that the minister's wife could take to strengthen her physical health:

1.

2.

3.

Use this space to make a list of actions that the minister and his wife could take to strengthen emotional health:

1.

2.

3.

Let's focus on physical health first. Both husband and wife can make some healthful changes. First, each of them should get a complete physical "wellness" exam to determine what, if any, medical conditions, such as high blood pressure or obesity, may need treatment. In the event the results are good in the wellness exam, then each of them would do well to start a regular program of physical exercise to assist them with stress management and weight management. Additionally, Rev. Dogood would be wise to continue the counseling and therapy he began in the rehabilitation program in order to address issues of possible addiction.

Regarding the emotional health of Rev. Dogood and Mrs. Dogood, there are several possible best practices that could be implemented. When both Rev. Dogood and Mrs. Dogood begin to pay more attention to their physical health perhaps their emotional states will also improve. Rev. Dogood could begin to set aside a regular day of Sabbath that he uses for rest and renewal instead

Notes:

of sermon preparation or hospital visits. This will need to be planned with the congregation so there can be a clear understanding of the time boundaries that are needed and an understanding of how visitation will be covered if necessary. Both Rev. Dogood and Mrs. Dogood might benefit from counseling for stress management and time management. Mrs. Dogood may benefit from counseling related to addiction issues to better understand what led to Rev. Dogood's drinking problems.

Power, Service, and Best Practices

Briefly review the cases described in this chapter to see how each clergyperson utilized the power of his or her status as a minister to influence each congregation. What were the results of their decisions and actions? Did some of the ministers use the power of their role to promote the best interests of their congregations? Did some of the ministers use the power of their role to enhance or advance their own personal desires and self-interests? What were the results for the congregations in which the minister always acted in the best interests of ministry, as compared to the results for the congregations in which the minister's first priority was his or her own best interests? Hopefully, these studies clearly show how easily ministers can persuade themselves, and others, that the ministers' own wellbeing is synonymous with the congregation's mission and how dangerous and costly this can be.

A most persuasive graduate school professor made valiant efforts to teach our class that the true nature of the power of the minister is displayed when the minister uses her best efforts on behalf of another. The power of the minister is diminished whenever she uses it for anything other than service for others. Although I don't remember much of the Greek language, my professor forever imprinted one phrase in my memory, *imitatio dei*, or "imitate God". To remember *imitatio dei* is to remember that serving another person—putting the other's needs ahead of my own—is to share God's own power and presence with another. To remember *imitatio dei* is to remember that our work in serving others is *always* an act of worship and *never* an act of self-aggrandizement.

As a final exercise, use the example of Hypothetical Case 1 below and take another look at the other Hypothetical Cases in this chapter. Review each case and develop a summary of the practices each clergy person could have employed personally and professionally to best reflect *imitatio dei* as his or her guiding principle.

Hypothetical Case 1: Clergy must serve the best interests of the congregation by:

1. keeping in mind the long-term staffing and financial needs of the congregation, and not focusing on an expedient option that goes unexamined, like the seeming convenience of allowing the business manager to be the sole signatory on accounts

2. calling for annual audits as a standard procedure, calling for appropriate receipts and records for all reimbursements of expenses and applying these procedures to all persons seeking reimbursements, maintaining a checks and balances system for counting offerings, and for managing all church financial accounts.

Hypothetical Case 2: Clergy must serve the best interests of the congregation by:

1.

2.

Notes:

IMITATIO DEI:
to reflect the image
of God to all.

Notes:

Hypothetical Case 3: Clergy must serve the best interests of the congregation by:

1.

2.

Hypothetical Case 4: Clergy must serve the best interests of the congregation by:

1.

2.

Interpersonal Relationships

Every relationship between a minister and another person includes a dimension of power. It is beyond the scope of this resource to give an exhaustive treatment of the psychological dynamics involved in the interpersonal relationships of ministers and parishioners. However, there are a couple of aspects of relationships that we certainly must understand thoroughly. The balance of power between or among parties in relationship is a crucial factor to understand when we must make ethical decisions about appropriate behaviors by ministers toward others. The interpersonal boundaries existing between parties to a relationship are another important factor that must be recognized. Every minister is involved every day in a wide variety of interpersonal relationships each of which may have somewhat different boundaries between the parties and a different balance of power for the parties. Think about the most common interpersonal relationships a minister participates in:

- Minister and parishioner
- Minister and church staff member
- Minister and church volunteer
- Minister and spouse
- Minister and peer
- Minister and child

There are also a variety of dimensions within each of these relationships. For example, on any given day, the minister may be involved

Notes:

SEE JAMES 3:1-13 for a scriptural description of the consequences of violations of boundaries of conversation!

with parishioners who are seeking counseling, or who are in the hospital, or a parishioner who is grieving the death of a loved one, or a parishioner who is in prison.

What interpersonal boundaries must the minister consider in any of these? Between the minister and any of these parishioners, the minister will need to establish, or recognize and maintain boundaries that define the conversation between them, the places where they meet, and the times at which they meet. It may seem too simplistic to describe the important interpersonal boundaries in such straightforward terms; but, the truth is that these terms actually encompass the breadth of our ministerial relationships.

Boundaries of conversation are usually mentioned in regard to the maintenance of confidentiality of information shared by the parishioner with the minister. Understanding the meaning of confidentiality is vital for the minister. When a parishioner seeks spiritual guidance on matters that are troubling to him or her the conversation is not to be shared with any other. State laws and the polity of many denominations recognize this as the clergy-penitent privilege and honor this except in circumstance of child abuse. Clergy persons are well trained to share with the parishioner seeking spiritual counseling that confidentiality will be maintained but that the clergy person will not keep reports of child abuse secret. By sharing such a policy at the beginning of the counseling relationship, the clergy person establishes clear boundaries and gives the parishioner control over what he or she chooses to share in the conversation.

However, there are other boundaries of conversation that are also called for in every day circumstances. Ministers must not be the "gossips" of the congregation or the community. We must not share in public what we may learn about any individuals or families through our visits with them or our conversations with friends.

Indiscriminate or imprudent comments made about members of the congregation or of the community will virtually always result in unhappiness, if not harm. Indiscriminate use of language, such as slang terminology and even profanity, reflects poorly on the minister's professional image and diminishes the strength of his or her leadership. After all, ministers are expected to be skilled and fluent communicators who need not rely on four-letter words! Humor in conversation must be carefully considered and appropriate boundaries recognized. Even if I know an amusing story about a parishioner and believe it would be appreciated by her friend if I shared it, it is not my story to tell. For example, one day I wore a new jacket to a luncheon with a group of my friends, including several clergy persons and a few persons that I had not met previously. I thought I had taken all the tags off the jacket before leaving home, but I missed one. At the luncheon I was introduced to several of the new folks before we sat down to the meal. One of my friends slipped a note to me saying, "You still have a tag on the sleeve of your jacket!" We had a chuckle about that and I was thankful that she told me, rather than just letting me go all day without knowing. I would have been embarrassed later to find that everyone saw that tag except me. That's an amusing, humorous story that I am perfectly willing to tell about myself. However, it is my story to tell—to confess that I got dressed in a hurry that day and to express my gratitude for a good enough friend to point out the tag I hadn't seen. It might not seem so amusing if I discovered that my friend told lots of other friends about it after lunch instead of telling me first! Humor isn't really humor if it is at the expense of someone else. Humor at the expense of parishioners is a violation of appropriate boundaries of conversation.

Boundaries of place must be established in our professional interpersonal relationships. The minister must take the lead in this regard. When you begin in a new church assignment, communicate your boundaries. For example,

Notes:

Notes:

if you are willing to meet with parishioners for counseling in your church office, let that be known along with the hours during which you can be available. If you are a youth minister, establish practices for meeting with the youth, individually or collectively that demonstrate your commitment to their safety and yours. Meeting with members of the youth group in a public place, or in your office with a door open, makes a clear statement that you are available without jeopardizing their security. No matter what meeting you are planning, arrange to use a space that will not isolate you and the others or create any impression that the meeting is a secret.

Boundaries of time exist in our interpersonal relationships. Ministers must maintain reasonable boundaries of time in order to accomplish our many tasks as well as to honor the other's responsibilities and commitments. Consideration of time is important when planning pastoral visits in homes as well as in visits to those in the hospital. On a visit to a family's home for a barbecue dinner and a Sunday School party, it would probably be absurd to think that the visit should last no more than fifteen minutes. On a visit to a parishioner who is hospitalized and recovering from serious illness, limiting the visit to only a few minutes may be entirely appropriate.

A wise doctor who was himself recovering from cancer and hospitalized for a brief time once told me, "I'm thankful that you've come to visit and I'll be thankful if you come again tomorrow, but I want you to know that when I say, 'Thanks for coming, I really appreciate it', that is my signal to you that I'm ready for you to leave." As a doctor, he had many patients over the years who told him that the pastor had come to visit and stayed too long! He also reminded me that although hospitals will usually welcome a minister for a visit even if "visiting hours" are over, it is always appreciated for the minister to check with the nurses' station before entering the patient's room.

BOUNDARIES OF TIME
and place will guide our relationships.

Visits with those who are grieving the death of a loved one are a frequent responsibility of ministers. Initially, the minister will visit with the family members to plan for the funeral or memorial service, and this could be a lengthy visit. Subsequent visits with family members need not be as lengthy.

In counseling sessions, keep to a schedule that is shared with the parishioner in the beginning. Usually, a session will be fifty minutes or less. In addition, set a limit to the number of sessions. Be clear at the outset to avoid confusion or hurt feelings later on.

Finally, boundaries of touch in our interpersonal relationships must be considered here. As the author of *Safe Sanctuaries: Reducing the Risk of Child Abuse in Church*, I have consulted with many ministers and many congregations in designing their ministries with children, youth, and vulnerable adults. In every congregation, the leaders ask whether preventing abuse requires that we prohibit hugging the children or even changing diapers in the nursery. That question is born out of our serious concern for the safety of children and youth within our ministries. That question also demonstrates that when ministers and parishioners begin thinking about appropriate boundaries of touch in our interpersonal relationships, it isn't harmful sexualized touching that first comes to mind.

The gospels report stories of Jesus offering healing, compassionate, and comforting touch to both children and adults. As ministers we will have many opportunities in the course of our work to do the same. We can share compassionate and comforting touch with others without introducing a sexualized dimension to our relationships. We can protect ourselves from misunderstandings, false allegations, and painful conflict by adopting strong and appropriate boundaries of touch in all that we do.

Notes:

JESUS OFFERED HEALING compassionate, and comforting touch, and we may follow His model.

Notes:

In a normal workday, a minister may shake hands with a visitor, hold the hand of a hospital patient while saying a prayer, and hug a church member at a fellowship dinner. Would any of these actions be inappropriate? Not necessarily but the answer may depend on the specific circumstances. These touches, when performed without any sexualization of the behavior, would most likely be perceived by the other person as comforting, welcoming, and compassionate behavior. Another key would be that these touches were delivered in open and public settings such as the fellowship dinner instead of isolated or secret locations.

Let's think a little more about the hug given to a parishioner at a fellowship dinner. We know there are different types of hugs. Some are friendly, some are sexualized. We must be able to communicate our care without giving an impression that we are seeking to develop a sexual dimension to our relationship with those we touch. Have you ever worked in a church summer camp with children or youth? If so, you know that every day brings a lot of hugs between campers and counselors, campers and campers, and counselors and counselors. Hugs at camp are meant to convey the joy we share at being together in God's beautiful outdoor world with friends old and new. How can we assure this is the message our touch communicates?

When I led the training for the summer camp counselors and staff at our church's camp, I suggested that giving each other and the campers "side hugs" would be a helpful way to communicate an appropriate message. Hug me by putting your arm around my shoulders, with the other members of the group present, and I can feel your support and friendship without any question that you are trying to sexualize that touch. Hug me by putting your arms around my neck and pressing your whole body up against mine at a time when no other members of the group are nearby, and I might worry that you are trying to communicate some sexual meaning through this touch. During that training session, we practiced "side hugs" with each other and talked about how some campers might be more open to this kind of touch than others. Honestly, the same concerns and concepts are applicable to every instance in our ministries when we offer touch or receive touch that is meant to convey joy, enthusiasm, compassion, or hospitality.

We must establish and maintain appropriate boundaries of touch not only to guide our own behavior but also to guide the behavior of those we are in relationship with. For example, we model for others the touches that are acceptable to us by the touch we offer. If I, as a camp counselor, give "side hugs" regularly to others, then others can become comfortable giving me "side hugs". The same is true for the ways we model and demonstrate our boundaries of touch in all our professional interpersonal relationships.

How are the boundaries of touch different for us in our dating or romantic relationships than they are for us in our relationships with parishioners? I doubt that we want to limit our boundaries of touch to "side hugs" in our romantic relationships! However, even in our marriages, we must intentionally decide what our public boundaries of touch will be with our spouses. Are we comfortable holding hands with each other? Do we feel it is appropriate to greet each other with a brief kiss in public? I once belonged to a Sunday School class where there was one man who greeted his wife with a kiss on the lips every time he sat down beside her. He tried to give all the women in the class a similar kiss every week by positioning himself near the door and acting as the unofficial "greeter". He seemed completely unaware of how uncomfortable this was for the other women and their spouses. On my first visit in the class he caught me by surprise. On my second visit, I intentionally kept enough space between us that a kiss of any kind would have

Notes:

Notes:

NO MEANS NO!

been impossible. On my third visit, he tried again and I said, "I'm glad to see you, but I reserve my kisses for my husband." The result was that some of the other women in the class felt more confident in keeping a little more distance from him and he simply continued to shower his wife with kisses. At the time, I responded to him based on my personal attitudes about public displays of affection. However, in the eyes of the class members, I had responded as the "minister's wife", and the response I gave was doubly effective. Everyone seemed to be liberated to maintain their own personal boundaries of touch because the "minister's wife" was doing exactly that. The boundaries of touch that we keep as ministers with our parishioners and our family members are persuasive models of behavior, maybe more persuasive than we sometimes realize! However, we are also instructed by the models set by our parishioners. Here is an example. When my daughter was four years old, we moved to a new congregation. She was not what you would describe as a shy child but she was careful in new situations. In the first few weeks many members of the congregation approached her to say hello and almost all of them enveloped her in a hug. She didn't try to resist them but she didn't return the embraces with enthusiasm. One man took a different approach. Compared to my four-year-old daughter, Leon was very tall. He knelt down on his knee so he could look her in the eye. He said, "Hello, Kathryn. My name is Leon. I'm glad you and your mom have joined my church. May I give you a hug?" Then, he actually waited for her permission. Kathryn looked at him and said, "No, thank you. I have to go to Sunday School." Leon accepted her response. He chuckled and she went down the hall to her classroom. It wasn't long before Kathryn began to look for Leon to say hello to him with a smile and eventually with a hug. They remain friends to this day. That encounter taught me how to model caring, compassionate, and respectful boundaries of touch with persons of all ages.

Resources of Power Within Interpersonal Relationships

Power in a relationship is derived from a number of different sources. In evaluating the balance of power between parties, we need to consider factors such as the ages of the parties, the educational levels attained by the parties, the gender(s) of the parties, the professional credentials of the parties, the marital status of the parties, the health status of the parties, the economic status of the parties, and many others. For example, if I want to understand the balance of power between two members of the church staff, I could consider many factors such as the ages of each, the length of time each has been on the staff, the professional credentials of each, the gender of each, the previous work experiences of each. If one of these staff members is ten to fifteen years older than the other, has more advanced education and professional credentials, and has been on the staff a few more years than the other, then I might conclude that the balance of power tilts in favor of the older staff member in some circumstances. If one of these two staff members is a clergy person and the other is a lay person, then the balance will often tilt in favor of the clergy person, even if the other staff member is older and has been on the staff longer. Why? In our society the clergy status has historically been imbued with such a high level of respect from parishioners and community members alike that persons holding this status are routinely assumed to be persons who are worthy of our trust, devotion, and even obedience. Sometimes the belief in the clergy person's integrity and trustworthiness is so strong that it will persist against overwhelming evidence to the contrary. Thus, clergy status is a source of power in the interpersonal relationships between clergy and lay persons. Ministers who have a clear understanding of this truth will be better equipped to make appropriate ethical decisions involving relationships. Awareness of this power must guide us to behave with integrity and without abusing the trust placed in us.

Ministers need to understand the balance of power that is operative in each committee, each class, and each fellowship group. Understanding that the chairperson of the committee is not necessarily the most influential member in some situations can mean the difference in success or failure of any particular project. In some congregations, the most powerful person—the one whose advice is always sought and whose opinion is always trusted—is not on any committee and holds no office. The minister needs to know such persons and to understand the specific resources of power possessed by them in order to know how and why their influence is so strong.

These leaders, when they behave with integrity and put the best interests of the congregation ahead of their individual interests, can be dynamic allies with the minister. Conversely, difficulty can arise when the minister fails to understand the resources of power of these leaders or when these leaders choose to use their considerable resources for purposes other than the best interests of the congregation.

Other factors such as race, ethnicity, and language proficiency can affect the balance of power in relationships. Most of us today live in multi-cultural, multi-racial, and multi-ethnic communities where it is possible to observe the effects of these types of factors on the balance of power in interpersonal relationships. Let me share an illustration. I know a family who immigrated to the U.S. from Cuba in the mid 1950s. In Cuba, members of the family were lawyers, doctors, and highly respected members of the community. Ethnically, this family is Hispanic. In Cuba, they were certainly proficient in the dominant language, which was Spanish. They immigrated to the United States to escape the oppressive conditions that were developing in Cuba in that era and find better opportunities for their children. Once they arrived here, they studied to meet the requirements for becoming United States citizens. They learned to speak fluently the dominant language here, English, but Spanish remained their "first" language. Although they have worked diligently and been successful by many measures, they did not become lawyers and doctors here. In their adopted homeland, they have not been members of majority groups, such as English-speaking Caucasian men and women, and that fact has had ramifications for the interpersonal relationships they have had in the community where they live. They are highly respected members of the community, just as they were in Cuba. However, by giving up the resource of being leaders in the majority group, someone looking at the situation from the outside would say they gave up a measure of power. Members of the family would be more likely to say that the measure of power they gained with freedom was greater than the measure of power they left behind.

Clergy status has been found to be a source of power within interpersonal relationships in many cultures and ethnic groups, not just in Hispanic or Caucasian groups. Across the board, ministers in every community must be aware of the high level of integrity that is expected of us and the high level of trust that is placed in us as we make all kinds of decisions. If we make professional choices and decisions that place the best interests of our parishioners ahead of our personal interests we will be less likely to make choices that will abuse the trust that has been given us.

I have been involved with congregations that could be described as Hispanic, African-American, Asian, Caucasian, multi-ethnic, and multi-cultural. In every one of these congregations, one thing has been constant. The clergy members of the congregation were highly respected and admired simply because they were clergy. Parishioners believe that the ministers are dedicated to serving the gospel and therefore ministers will always act to put the best interests of others ahead of their individual best interests. The strength of this belief can

Notes:

Notes:

sometimes keep parishioners from seeing any signs or clues of clergy misconduct. The strength of this belief can also lead to parishioners blaming victims, rather than listening to reports of clergy misconduct.

Hypothetical Cases

Let's review several types of interpersonal relationships that ministers often encounter. These include counseling relationships, visiting parishioners in the hospital or at home, and friendships with parishioners, dating relationships between a minister and parishioner, and staff relationships.

Hypothetical Case No. 1

Here is a hypothetical example of how the opinion leader's power resources were used unwisely to promote individual goals rather than the best interests of the congregation. I'll call the opinion leader Ms. Leader. The church council met in March and voted to find a Summer Intern to work with the youth group and lead the summer programs. The pastor announced in the worship service that they were looking for an Intern and would be accepting applications for this position. The next day, Ms. Leader called the church council chairman to say that she knew the perfect candidate for the Summer Intern position: her grandson, John. She said he was completing his first year of college, needed a summer job, and since he had been a member of the youth group before he went to college, he had an advantage of already knowing everyone. The council chairman, Mr. Council, told her they would prefer to have someone more than one year older than the senior high youth but if her grandson wanted to apply, they would consider his application. Ms. Leader contacted Pastor Smith, every member of the church council and every member of the selection committee to share her brilliant idea for filling the Summer Intern position. At the first meeting of the selection committee, the members were prepared to review all the applications they had received and decide which candidates would be invited to interview. A dozen applications had been sent to the committee. However, before the committee got very far in examining the applications, one member said, "Wouldn't it be easier if we just offered the job to John? We already know him. He is a good kid and besides, we all know how much Ms. Leader wants him to have the job." A majority of the committee members agreed and decided to offer the position to John without even having an interview with him.

John became the Summer Intern. He also began dating one of the girls in the group who was going to be a high school senior when school resumed at the end of the summer. Pastor Smith instructed him that dating a member of the youth group was inappropriate and unprofessional. Pastor Smith believed that John stopped dating the girl even though rumors floated around that they were still seeing each other.

When the summer internship ended, John returned to college. The girl he had dated moved away. The next spring, she returned to the community with a high school diploma and a baby. She admitted that John was the father of her child. It didn't take very long for word to spread through the congregation.

Ms. Leader strongly denied her grandson was the child's father. She made it a point to talk with everyone she could. In each conversation she insinuated that the girl was "bad" or "making this up" or "wanted to get revenge against her grandson because he stopped dating her." The more she talked, the more the congregation became divided. Pastor Smith tried having a conversation with Ms. Leader, but she insisted that he should be taking up for John and making public statements of

support for John. Pastor Smith tried to have a conversation with John, but his overtures were repeatedly refused. Ms. Leader took her version of events to others outside of the congregation and added that if Pastor Smith had adequately supervised the church staff last summer, none of this could have happened.

Each Sunday that passed brought more conflict and division to the congregation. Those who believed Ms. Leader began to sit together on one side of the sanctuary and those who believed the girl sat together on the other side. Those who believed Ms. Leader began to withdraw from groups and committees that had members who believed the girl. Fewer visitors attended worship. The offerings given each week and the members' attendance began to shrink noticeably.

Pastor Smith exhausted himself trying to facilitate and achieve reconciliation and restoration of good relationships in the congregation and in the community. Finally, after several years, he resigned from his position at the church. He left with the feeling that he had been an abject failure as pastor.

This is a sad example of the consequences of an opinion leader's inappropriate use of her resources of power. It is also a very sad example of the consequences of the pastor and church council not understanding clearly how submission to Ms. Leader's power would lead to devastating consequences for the congregation.

Hypothetical Case No. 2

Sarah Clark was a member of First Church. Rev. Goodman was the pastor. In the spring of 2005, Sarah went to Rev. Goodman for marital counseling. The first appointment was late one afternoon in May in the pastor's office at the church. Sarah felt a little better after their meeting and she asked for another appointment.

After the second appointment, she began meeting with Rev. Goodman at least once a week. This continued for eight or nine weeks. At the end of one of their appointments in the pastor's office, Sarah reached out and hugged Rev. Goodman. He was surprised but didn't comment on it.

The next session seemed to last longer than usual. Sara seemed to have a lot of questions for him about his hobbies and interests outside of church. She was much more talkative than she had been in previous sessions. At the end of the session, he was very surprised when she reached out to hug him, as she had in the previous session. This time she held on to him so long that he felt like he had to pull away and move toward the office door.

Even though he felt a little uncomfortable about the hugs, Rev. Goodman kept the next appointment. He found himself telling her about his frustrations with the congregation. She felt honored that her pastor would share his personal feelings with her. He had mentioned to her when she first met with him that he was not a professional counselor; but, he seemed so insightful and charming that she just kept making more appointments. After several more sessions, she called Rev. Goodman and suggested that they meet at the local coffee shop instead of at the church. He agreed to this.

Sarah told Rev. Goodman that she considered their appointments the highlight of her week. She admitted that while she had been on vacation with her husband and children recently she had wished she was with him. He felt flattered by all her attention. Then, something unexpected happened. Sarah came to the church and told him that her husband was being transferred by his employer to a different town about fifty miles away and the whole family would be moving very soon. Rev. Goodman expressed his sorrow to lose Sarah and her

family as members of the church and offered to suggest a couple of churches for them to visit in the new location.

Sarah called Rev. Goodman to say that she was terribly lonely and would like to meet him. He agreed to meet her at a restaurant about halfway between the two towns. He gave her a note card with the name and contact information for a professional family counselor in her new town and suggested that she make an appointment with the counselor. He told her that he was concerned for her. He told her it would be better for her to have a local counselor because he would not be able to travel to meet with her any longer. He gave her a hug as they left the restaurant and walked her to her car.

Several weeks later, Rev. Goodman received a call from the pastor of New Church, Rev. Smith. Rev. Smith thought Rev. Goodman should know that Sarah had come to him and made allegations of misconduct against Rev. Goodman and that she was extremely angry. Rev. Goodman was shocked by this and cannot understand why Sarah would be angry with him.

How would you, as a minister, have handled Sarah's request for counseling differently?

1.

2.

At what points in this story was Rev. Goodman presented with ethical dilemmas? List the ethical dilemmas here.

1.

2.

3.

What would you recommend as the best standard practices for ministers when parishioners request counseling appoints? List the best practices here.

1.

2.

3.

4.

Assume that you are the chairperson of the church's personnel committee. What practices would you suggest the committee adopt as standards and best practices for counseling by the pastor(s) on the staff? List the best practices here.

1.

2.

3.

4.

Hypothetical Case No. 3

Let's look at another type of situation. It is very common for seminary students to work in churches as youth ministry leaders. Every church's youth ministry will present opportunities that require decision-making based on mature judgment and strong ethical standards. The following hypothetical gives just one, of many, possible situations that occur in youth ministry.

Assume the following details. Wesley United Methodist Church has a very active youth ministry. There are nearly one hundred youth involved. The staff person

Notes:

responsible for youth ministry is a young man, John, who graduated from college a year ago. He is a first-year seminary student and a candidate for ordination in this annual conference. John has been working as the Youth Director for about six months. In addition to his duties with the youth, he is also expected to attend the weekly staff meetings. Bob, the Sr. Pastor, has welcomed him into the church and encouraged John to come to him anytime he needs anything.

One of the first programs John started for the youth was a Bible study group. The group meets in the evening at the home of one of the Senior High youth. The group meets at a different home each week. Although John has always made it a point to ask the host student's parents to be at home during the Bible study meeting, on several occasions the parents have been absent. Rather than disappoint the youth, John has gone ahead with the Bible study even though he was the only adult leader present. Every week at staff meeting, John reports that the Bible study is going well and the number of students is increasing steadily.

There has been one girl in the group who has seemed to need extra attention and John has reached out to her. Now and then she comes by the church to see him, in addition to seeing him at the Bible study. When she comes to see him at the church office, she doesn't ask him to listen to her problems. She just seems to be lonely. John has given her a ride home from the Bible study twice. Today, one of the regular adult leaders of the Sunday evening youth fellowship, Scott, came to see John. He told John that the girl has begun telling others in the Bible study group that she is dating John and they are carrying on an intimate relationship. John is shocked and frightened. He denies that he is dating the girl or that they have an intimate relationship, but he wonders how he can prove that. John thanks Scott for bringing this to his attention and asks for any suggestions Scott might have about how to handle the matter. Scott and John discussed the situation and concluded several things needed to be done.

What actions by John led to this situation? List the actions here.

1.

2.

3.

What best practices can John adopt to prevent this type of situation from developing in the future? List the best practices here.

1.

2.

3.

What best practices could Bob, the Sr. Pastor, have utilized that would have helped to prevent this type of situation? List the best practices here.

1.

2.

3.

Hypothetical Case No. 4

Billy Goldson was a good student in divinity school and received good evaluations from the churches where he worked as an intern. The bishop gave Billy

Notes:

LISTEN TO THE
children and youth!

an appointment, after graduation in June, to a large congregation where he was to be the Youth Minister. The bishop had great confidence that Billy would become highly successful.

Billy started off in the congregation enthusiastically. He made visits to the homes of all the members of the youth group. He planned lots of fun activities. He played the guitar and offered inspirational devotions at every meeting of the youth group. He made it a point to tell the youth that he was always available if any of them needed someone to talk to.

Within just a few months, the parents who had been volunteer leaders when Billy arrived had been relieved of their duties. Billy said he knew they had worked hard and needed a break so he would take over the complete leadership and supervision of the youth. Some of the volunteers were glad; but some thought it was a little strange.

By springtime, the parents began to notice that Billy was inviting the boys to his home frequently to play video games, watch movies, or "just hang out" in the evenings. No other adults were included. Some parents spoke to the senior minister, Rev. One, and asked that Billy be advised to include other adults in these meetings.

Rev. One did instruct Billy to include other adults in the youth meetings, no matter where the meetings were held. He also advised Billy that meeting the youth—boys and girls—at church would be better than meeting them in his home. Billy stopped inviting the boys to his home for a while. He set up video games in his office and told the boys they could come to the church after school any afternoon.

By the end of Billy's first year in this congregation, the Senior Pastor had received several reports from parents that their sons no longer were willing to participate in youth ministry. The reason being given by the boys was that Billy made them uncomfortable. Rev. One told Billy of these concerns. He instructed Billy to include adult volunteers in all aspects of youth ministry. The parents agreed to volunteer in the programs again.

Billy had stopped having the boys over to his home. He accepted adult volunteer leaders in the ministry. But then, he began sending text messages to some of the boys, inviting them to meet him at various places. Usually, he invited just one youth at a time to meet him. Some of the boys simply ignored the text invitations; but that just seemed to make Billy send them more messages. Some of the boys answered the messages and met Billy at the church, or the local movie theater, or other places. The parents noticed the text messaging charges going up on their phone bills but they didn't recognize Billy's number at first. Finally, one of the boys asked his father for help. He felt stressed out, anxious, and didn't know how to stop Billy's incessant messages.

Mr. Smith checked his cell phone records and found that in a month's time, his son had received nearly a thousand text messages from Billy. His son told him that he had gone to see Billy at church several times, just to try to get Billy to leave him alone. Mr. Smith talked with some other parents. They all checked their cell phone records and found similar information. The boys all reported the same things—incessant messages, demanding more and more time with them, and when they were together, making the boys feel physically vulnerable and uncomfortable. The parents went to Rev. One and demanded that Billy be removed from the Youth Minister's position.

Rev. One called Billy in to his office and asked to see Billy's appointment calendar for the previous two months. The calendar had appointments noted for nearly

every afternoon with a different boy each day. Billy said these were counseling appointments with youth who were having difficulties at home or at school. Rev. One then shared the reports that had been brought by the parents. Billy's explanation of the text messages was that he used texting to counsel the youth when they couldn't meet in person. Rev. One told Billy that it would not be in the best interests of his career to continue in this congregation because the families had lost confidence in him.

Rev. One asked the bishop not to reappoint Billy for the coming year. The bishop met with Billy and informed him that he would be appointed to another congregation as Youth Minister. Bishop Masters advised him to conduct himself professionally and not to let any rumors get started in the new congregation.

Billy started to work in the new congregation and seemed to be following the bishop's advice. Rev. Two, the senior pastor in this congregation, was impressed with the effort Billy was making to get to know all the families. However, within a few months, Rev. Two began receiving reports from parents that Billy was seeking inappropriate meetings with the youth. When Rev. Two asked Billy about the concerns, Billy responded that he was counseling youth who were having troubles at home or at school and that the parents were just overreacting. The parents began to pay close attention to the events going on in youth ministry and several of them volunteered to be adult leaders. Billy tried to reject their offers.

Finally, the parents took their concerns to Rev. Two again and asked him to remove Billy from the youth minister position. Rev. Two notified Bishop Masters that the congregation did not want Billy reappointed there. Bishop Masters agreed that Billy would be sent to a new congregation in June.

Just a few months after beginning at the third church, a junior high boy in the youth group reported to his parents that Billy had assaulted him in Billy's office at the church. The parents were outraged. Instead of going back to the senior pastor, they retained an attorney and brought a lawsuit naming the church, Billy, and the bishop as defendant parties. The investigation conducted in preparation for trial showed that Billy may have engaged in sexual abuse of minors in all three congregations where he worked.

Let's think about the first congregation in this story. What best practices could have been utilized that would have reduced the likelihood that Billy would have been able to harm any of the youth? List your suggestions:

1.

2.

3.

4.

There are best practices that would be useful for the congregation to have used and additional best practices for Rev. One to have used. The congregation could have:

1. Maintained its core adult volunteer leadership, even though Billy said he didn't need them anymore. This would have provided ongoing supervision of both the youth and the new youth minister, minimizing the opportunities for isolation.
2. Given Billy a complete training and orientation in the congregation's Safe Sanctuaries® procedures including policies regarding counseling procedures such as

   • Meeting at the church during normal hours
   • Having counseling meetings when others are present nearby

75

Notes:

3. Given Billy a complete orientation to the church's policies for communication with the youth and families by phone, email, text messages, website, and any other media. The Youth Minister must be expected to use communication media responsibly, including following church policy on text messages, email, websites, and social networking such as Facebook, MySpace, Twitter, and others. If your congregation uses any of these communication media, then you really must develop policies and procedures regarding the types of information that can be shared acceptably! Then, educate all staff members and church members about responsible use. Furthermore, if your congregation has website and social networking pages that it uses for communication, then you would be well advised to have every staff member, including the ministers, sign covenants acknowledging the policies and agreeing to abide by the policies.

There are several best practices that Rev. One could have used for effective supervision of Billy. List your suggestions:

1.

2.

3.

First, since Billy was serving in his first full time ministerial appointment after finishing seminary, Rev. One could have set up a regular schedule of meetings with him to guide his development of professional skills. Some of those meetings might well have included some of the volunteer leaders and served as planning meetings for upcoming events and activities.

WOULD YOU BE A
mentor for a new
clergy person?

Second, Rev. One and the district superintendent, could have required Billy to participate in a peer study group where he would have regularly been afforded the opportunity to learn from others in similar situations as well as from others more experienced than he.

Third, Rev. One could have engaged the church's staff parish relations committee in regular meetings with Billy for updates and evaluation, rather than leaving his evaluation to one meeting at the end of the year.

Fourth, Rev. One could have very specifically instructed Billy regarding his behavior and the changes that were expected, such as no text messages to youth without parental permission. His instructions and advice should be included in the church's file and in the report made to the district superintendent and/or bishop.

Think about the bishop in this story. When Bishop Masters heard from Rev. One that the congregation did not want Billy returned for a second year, was there anything he might have done to change the ultimate outcome in the second and third churches? For the sake of this study, let's assume that Billy was not a sexual predator and that the complaints made against him involved possible interpersonal boundary violations but not allegations of child abuse. How could the bishop have worked with Billy and with the second congregation to achieve a better outcome? List your suggestions:

1.

2.

3.

Here are some possibilities: Provide Billy with continuing education focused on interpersonal boundaries and

Notes:

professional ethics in youth ministry. Keep a record of the continuing education completed. Provide Billy with a mentor and/or a covenant peer group of others engaged in youth ministry. Meet with the new congregation's staff parish committee to provide an introduction to Billy, his experience, and his skills. Encourage them to uphold their Safe Sanctuaries® procedures with all who work with the youth.

Let's assume that Billy was not a child abuser but was, in fact, a young man who was dedicated to youth ministry. What best practices could he have followed to better assure that he would not be falsely accused of inappropriate conduct?

1. Meet youth at the church for counseling appointments and be sure that some other adult(s) are aware of the meeting. Keep a calendar of scheduled appointments and record impromptu meetings as well.
2. Follow the church's policies regarding communication through media such as email, text messaging, and social networking. Specifically, have parental permission to communicate with each youth in these media.
3. Maintain a strong group of adult volunteers and train all of them in Safe Sanctuaries® procedures regularly.
4. Assign at least two adults for each ministry setting, and more than two for large groups.
5. Provide education for parents and for youth on topics such as appropriate interpersonal boundaries and using the internet safely.

There are surely other Safe Sanctuary® best practices that would be helpful to Billy, and other youth ministers. List the ones you think of:

1.

2.

3.

Any congregation that has a clergyperson who is focused on youth ministry is a fortunate congregation. We must do all that we can to support the nurture and professional development of them while we also demonstrate our dedication to the protection of the church's ability to continue in ministry with children, youth, and adults.

Hypothetical Case No. 5

Let's look at a type of situation that seems to occur frequently in congregations where the minister is not married. As a result of getting acquainted with the parishioners, the minister begins to develop personal relationships with some of them in addition to the professional relationships expected between the clergy person and the congregants.

Assume the following details. Pastor Joe was appointed to First Church and began working there a little more than a year ago. He is twenty-nine years old, has not been married, is charming and friendly toward all the parishioners, and has been readily accepted by the congregation. He lives in the parsonage. Many of the families in the church have invited Joe to dinner and he has enjoyed getting to know the members. Very shortly after arriving, Joe was invited to join the Rotary Club and become their chaplain. The church is growing under Joe's leadership. New members seem to be coming into the congregation on a regular basis.

The United Methodist Women meet at the church each month for Bible study, mission projects, and fellowship. Pastor Joe has been the Bible study leader for them several times. He is always glad to have a chance to work with them. The United Methodist Men also meet each

Notes:

BEWARE OF DUAL
relationships.

month and Pastor Joe attends their meetings and works along with them on their mission projects. Some of the men are on a softball team together and Pastor Joe has joined the team. The team plays on Saturday mornings.

About six months ago, Mrs. Smith came to Pastor Joe after the worship service and introduced him to Judy, her daughter. Judy had just returned to the community after being away for several years. Judy has a new job in town, is single, and Mrs. Smith says she's glad to have her daughter back in church. Judy has become a regular participant in worship and joined the United Methodist Women's group for young professionals. She has also joined the Rotary Club. Judy and Joe had numerous opportunities to get acquainted with each other and their friendship developed easily.

When the Rotary Club Annual Ball was approaching, Judy confided to her mother that she didn't want to attend without a date but she didn't know who to ask. Mrs. Smith suggested that she invite Pastor Joe. After all, she said, they were already friends and he probably didn't know anyone to invite either.

Judy and Pastor Joe went to the Ball together and enjoyed themselves. Since then, the friendship between them has deepened into a romantic relationship. Last week, Joe asked her to marry him. They haven't set a wedding date yet, but everyone in the congregation thinks that will be a happy event! Some of the guys on the softball team have started teasing him about planning a bachelor party.

Yesterday, Judy came to the church at lunchtime and told Joe she had something serious to talk about. Judy poured out a story of a traumatic event she experienced in college and said she has been having nightmares about it lately. She said she had believed that she had recovered from the trauma years ago and doesn't know what might be causing the nightmares now. Finally, she asked Joe for advice and his ideas for coping with the stress and anxiety she was suffering.

At this point, Judy and Pastor Joe have what can be described as dual relationships: the professional relationship of pastor and parishioner and a personal romantic relationship. Joe realized when he listened to Judy that he couldn't be objective as her pastor because he had such strong personal feelings for her.

What actions would you recommend that Joe take now in his role as Judy's pastor? List the actions here.

1.

2.

How can Joe best respond and appropriately differentiate between his roles as pastor and fiancé? List the best responses here.

1.

2.

When dual relationships develop between a pastor and parishioner, the personal relationship isn't always a romantic one. For example, Joe may have dual relationships with some of the members of the church softball team because he has developed close friendships with them. In congregations like First Church, it is common for the minister to develop dual relationships with at least some of the parishioners and it isn't necessarily wrong for that to happen. However, it is important for both parties to be aware of the dual nature of their relationship.

As we have discussed, in the professional relationship between minister and parishioner each party has

Notes:

different resources depending on a variety of factors that will affect the balance of power between them. The clergy person has power because the status of ordination confers a measure of power on the ordained individual. In the case described here, Joe has a measure of power, by being an ordained minister that made Judy believe he was a good person, before she had romantic feelings for him. She perceived him as one who was trustworthy and she saw him behaving with integrity over a period of time. Therefore, in their professional relationship, Joe was somewhat more powerful than Judy. In their personal relationship, the balance of power between them is likely to have been more equal after they developed romantic feelings for each other.

There is another change between the parties that we don't often think about until we are in a crisis situation. As a professional relationship becomes a personal relationship, the minister will find it more and more difficult to act in his or her professional role with the other individual. When a crisis occurs, such as the nightmares and anxiety that Judy developed, if we haven't thought about how to handle this aspect of our dual relationship, then achieving a healthy outcome is going to be harder than it otherwise might have been.

You don't have to be caught off guard by this type of crisis. You can, along with the other person in the relationship, think ahead. Realize that you can't be objective when a close friend, spouse, or relative needs a minister more than they need you in your personal capacity. Be ready to connect your relative or friend with another minister or therapist or counselor. Also be ready to avail yourself of counseling or assistance of another professional when you need to.

Let's think about another possible scenario involving Joe and Judy. Assume that they are a clergy couple. They are employed in separate churches. Joe's church is thriving and all the ministries are going well. Judy's church is not thriving and she is highly stressed by the declines in membership and giving. At home, all she can talk about is the problems at her church. She says she needs to tell Joe everything because it helps her calm down and because she wants his advice. Joe listens and does his best to respond helpfully. No matter what suggestions he makes or what guidance he offers, Judy remains extremely anxious. Joe has offered to go to see a counselor with her but Judy isn't willing to take that step.

How would you describe the boundaries in the personal and professional relationships between Joe and Judy? Judy is struggling in her professional role and is relying on Joe for professional advice. As a result, she is expecting him to function not only as husband but also as coach, counselor, and professional colleague.

Assume you are a clergy person who is a friend to both Joe and Judy. What suggestions would you make to Judy for addressing the challenges she faces at work?

List suggestions here:

1.

2.

What suggestions would you make to her for clarifying the boundaries between home and work?

List suggestions here:

1.

2.

Notes:

In addition, what would you suggest to Joe and Judy together for addressing the high stress levels being caused by Judy's work conditions?

List suggestions here:

1.

2.

3.

Possible suggestions for Judy could include seeking counseling from other pastors who have faced similar challenges; finding a coach or mentor for helping her develop or strengthen her leadership skills; continuing education courses focused on specific areas that could be helpful, such as financial management skills. In addition, you might suggest a new, or renewed physical exercise routine, and observing a regular time of individual Sabbath rest.

Clergy-Pentitent Privilege and Confidentiality Issues

Review Hypothetical Case 4. We only need to change this hypothetical slightly to be able to examine issues related to confidentiality and reporting child abuse. *The Book of Discipline 2008* of the United Methodist Church, in Paragraph 341.5 specifically states, "All clergy of the United Methodist Church are charged to maintain all confidences inviolate, including confessional confidences, except in the cases of suspected child abuse or neglect or in cases where mandatory reporting is required by civil law."

Let's say that one of the boys in the junior high youth group at the first church reported to Billy that his mother was abusing him but that he didn't want Billy to "do anything" except pray for him. Assume this congregation is located in a state with a statute that makes reporting child abuse mandatory if an adult has reasonable cause to believe that abuse is occurring or has occurred. Billy has some decisions to make. Best practices in this situation would mean that Billy must follow state law and make the report to the appropriate authorities. State law requires this and *The Book of Discipline* allows this. What about the fact that the youth doesn't want a report to be made? Billy, as a youth minister who offers to provide counseling for youth, must develop a best practice of always telling the youth that he is obligated by law to report abuse. Further, he can assure the youth that he will not make the report and leave the youth without assistance. Billy will also need to inform Rev. One that a report of child abuse needs to be made. He will need to document what is reported to him, what actions he takes to follow the statute, and what assistance, if any, he provides for the youth. In a situation such as this, it is crucial to understand that keeping records will help protect the youth, his family, Billy, Rev. One, and the congregation. Every state has a child abuse reporting statute that sets forth who must report abuse, how the reports are to be made, and what authorities are to receive and investigate reports of abuse. Many of these statutes make clergy persons mandatory reports. Therefore, all clergy and volunteers need to be trained every year on the requirements of the statutes currently in effect in their state. To find the statute for your state, simply contact your local family and children services office.

Let's change this hypothetical one more time. In the first congregation, a junior high boy's parents come to Rev. One to report that their son has been sexually abused by Billy. What are the parents required to do, according to state law? What is Rev. One required to do? The parents are reporting to Rev. One; however, the statute in their state probably requires them to report their son's injury to

Notes:

KNOW YOUR STATE'S child & elder abuse reporting statutes.

local law enforcement authorities or the department of family and children services. The actual investigation of criminal allegations must be handled by the law enforcement authorities. Rev. One will need to document the parents' report to him and he could offer to accompany them.

What must Rev. One do in the event that the parents ask for Billy to be immediately removed from youth ministry at the church? Suspending Billy from his duties pending the investigation is the best practice for the protection of the youth group members, for the church, and for Billy, even if the parents haven't actually requested it. Rev. One must suspend Billy from further contact with the youth to insure that no new incidents will occur and to insure that no occasions for possibly false allegations occur. Rev. One and the staff parish committee must document these actions. Rev. One must also notify the district superintendent and Bishop Masters of the situation immediately. Experience has taught me that district superintendents and bishops do not appreciate being informed first by news media of situations such as this!

Let's assume in this hypothetical that Billy is arrested and charged with a crime against a child. Is the criminal prosecution the only prosecution of a complaint that needs to be carried out? Our denomination allows for a judicial complaint procedure to be followed, in addition to the secular criminal prosecution. In fact, remember that the parents who first reported Billy to Rev. One asked that he be removed from ministry. The secular process cannot achieve that outcome for it has no authority to remove Billy from the clergy. Only the church complaint procedure can achieve that. Therefore, it becomes important for the church to follow its judicial complaint process and resolve the complaint. The United Methodist Church's procedures are clearly detailed in *The Book of Discipline of the United Methodist Church 2008*. The procedures of other denominations are articulated in similar denominational resources.

Guidelines for Ethical Behavior

In summary, a review of these hypothetical situations leads to some very basic lessons for successful interpersonal relationships for ministry professionals. As ministers, we will very often find ourselves in situations that give us opportunities to touch others, spiritually, emotionally, and physically. By approaching each of these opportunities with the vision of *imitatio dei* we will be guided to offer the same compassionate care and concern to others that Christ modeled in his relationships.

Recently, my adult Bible study class studied the Old Testament, including the Ten Commandments. One of our members noted that only two commandments are phrased in positive terms: Remember the Sabbath and keep it holy; and, Honor your father and mother. The remaining eight commandments are those often referred to as the "Thou shalt nots!" For the most part, the "Thou shalt nots" set parameters for our relationships with others. As we tried to think of a way to summarize or paraphrase them to be more easily remembered, I shared the revision I learned from my dad, "If it isn't yours, don't touch it."

Imitatio dei and "If it isn't yours, don't touch it" are succinctly descriptive terms we can easily call to mind when we are making choices and decisions. Each of these can guide our relationships with money as well as our relationships with other persons of all ages. When we touch another person in a selfish, angry, disrespectful, or abusive way, we are failing to touch as Christ would. When we touch the church's resources and assets for selfish purposes, we are failing to live as Christ would. Touching another person with gentleness and respect when invited to, as a parishioner sometimes offers an embrace to the minister after the worship service or as a child sometimes invites a hug, demonstrates the touch of Christ. "Touching" the resources of our congregation by

Notes:

IF IT ISN'T YOURS,
don't touch it!

Notes:

guiding the use of them for the mission and ministry of the church demonstrates to all that we are dedicated to the ethical principles of Christian stewardship.

IMITATIO DEI:
reflect God's character
to all the world.

Legal Costs of Ethical Failures

There are always costs and consequences of the decisions we make personally or professionally. The costs and consequences of failures to follow best practices in making professional decisions can be devastating for individuals and congregations. The hypothetical situations we have worked through in the previous chapters have illustrated that litigation is a very costly consequence. Unfortunately, it occurs frequently. Even when civil litigation is brought to a final resolution, we don't hear the participants say, "Wow, that was therapeutic!" Instead, the participants often leave the courthouse feeling disappointed and disillusioned by the church.

Litigation related to churches and their ministers or employees is framed as a "civil lawsuit" or "criminal charges". In the civil lawsuit the plaintiff makes allegations against one or more defendants claiming that the defendant's actions caused harm or injury to the plaintiff. The lawsuit usually seeks monetary compensation for the harm or injury suffered by the plaintiff.

It is not uncommon in the context of a civil lawsuit for multiple defendants to be named, such as the church, the individual employee who allegedly caused the injury, and the annual conference. Each named defendant might be found liable for some or all of the alleged harm. Each defendant generally needs individual legal representation.

Notes:

When the civil lawsuit is initiated, the defendants are notified and given thirty days in which to respond. However, the suit will probably not be resolved in a mere thirty days. Instead, depending on the complexity of the issues, getting to the final judgment of the lawsuit may take years.

When criminal charges are involved in a church situation, usually one or more defendants are accused of criminal acts, such as child abuse or theft. The defendant might be a minister, an employee of the church, or a volunteer at the church. The defendant will need a legal representative but it will not necessarily be the church's responsibility to provide or pay for that legal representation. If the defendant is found guilty of the criminal charge then a prison sentence is the likely result.

Some situations have resulted in civil litigation and criminal litigation happening simultaneously. For example, when a minister of the church is arrested because a report has been made that he has abused a child, then these charges can lead to a criminal conviction and a jail sentence for him. At the same time, the parents of the child victim may initiate a civil lawsuit against the minister, seeking monetary compensation for the injury suffered by the child. The civil lawsuit might also include the church as a defendant on the theory that if the minister had been adequately supervised in his work, then the child might not have been harmed. This type of litigation can take years for the achievement of a final resolution.

When a minister is accused of a crime, or a number of other offenses, he or she may be brought before the church's disciplinary body to answer the accusations. In The United Methodist Church, the charges are brought before the Committee on Investigation and possibly a church trial court. This type of complaint is usually

CRIMINAL LITIGATION
and civil litigation are not forms of therapy.

expected to be processed and resolved in approximately six months. The resolutions of this type of complaint can include a wide range of possibilities such as surrender of ordination credentials, suspension for a period of time, or a letter of reprimand. *The Book of Discipline* spells out the actual complaint procedures to be followed. Other denominations have similar resources for handling internal complaints.

Over the past decade, I have met many victims of clergy sexual abuse and misconduct who have initiated either church complaints or secular litigation against the clergy offenders and the churches where they were employed. Some of these individuals tried to make church complaints rather than initiating secular litigation. When the church authorities listened carefully to the complainant and processed the complaint according to the established denominational procedures, in a reasonable length of time, often the result was that the complainant accepted the resolution as an appropriate closure of the complaint and was then less likely to pursue secular litigation. When the church authorities refused to listen or to process the complaint, the victims sometimes turned to secular litigation in frustration.

There are some costs involved in processing a complaint against a minister through the annual conference's or denomination's complaint procedure. The United Methodist procedures, as set forth in the *Book of Discipline* (Nashville: United Methodist Publishing House, 2008) will require the investment and use of time by the parties to the complaint, the bishop, the district superintendent, the members of the committee who will hear the complaint, and those who assist the parties. The requirements of processing the complaint in a limited amount of time will probably necessitate that all of those involved rearrange their schedules to meet the deadlines prescribed in *The Book of Discipline*.

Notes:

Notes:

A JUST RESOLUTION
can be sought.

The Book of Discipline allows for the use of a process seeking a just resolution of complaints by which the parties can be assisted by "a trained, impartial third party facilitator(s) or mediator(s) in reaching an agreement satisfactory to all parties." (*The Book of Discipline*, Nashville: United Methodist Publishing House, 2008, p. 285, Paragraph 361.1b). This can be initiated at any time during the pendency of a complaint, investigation, or trial. The process for seeking a just resolution is similar to the process of mediation in civil litigation. This, too, involves costs associated with the time required to complete a just resolution process. There may also be costs associated with retaining the trained facilitator to lead the process. However, my experience in civil litigation and the church complaint procedures has proven that the costs of this type of just resolution process are well worth the expenditure.

The just resolution process leads to a written statement of resolution that includes all terms and conditions. When the just resolution process is utilized effectively, the complainant can receive a satisfactory sense of having been listened to by the church leaders. Additionally, the complainant knows that the respondent has, or will be held accountable and what specific form(s) that accountability will take. In fact, all the parties will have full information through the just resolution process.

Ministers who are involved in a complaint process, or the just resolution process, either as complainant, respondent, or member of the investigation committee, find it to be an intense experience. There are some who have experienced both the church complaint procedure and the civil litigation process. They attest to the difficulties involved in each context. However, they attest to the fact that within the church complaint procedure there is greater opportunity to process the complaint to finality in a shorter period of time. The complainant benefits from timely resolution, the congregation and the annual conference benefit from timely resolution, and the respondent also benefits. When a complaint process has been completed within the church context, participants have been heard to say that they believed they had experienced the church acting as a true community of disciples would act.

When a complaint is taken to the secular courthouse for resolution, the costs to the parties' time can be much greater. Expenses of legal representation for the complainant can be prohibitive with no guarantee that they will be paid by the defendant/respondent. The individual respondent may have expenses for legal representation. The church and the annual conference may be named as additional defendants and thus, will face expenses for legal representation. Expenses of legal representation, unless provided for through the church's liability insurance coverage, can easily run into tens of thousands of dollars out of the church's budget. The ability to preserve confidentiality is also limited in civil litigation, given that court records are generally public records.

Complainants have shared with me that civil litigation is the last resort for them for another reason unrelated to time and legal fees. Civil lawsuits can result in the court or the jury awarding the complainant a monetary amount as compensation for their harm or injury; but, money is not what the complainant truly wants in cases of clergy misconduct. The complainant truly wants the clergy person to be prevented from perpetrating any further harm and the civil courts generally cannot provide this outcome.

Courts and juries have great difficulty determining a monetary amount that sufficiently compensates a victim of clergy sexual misconduct. Difficulty with this task does not lead a jury to minimize its award. Jury verdicts have exceeded a million dollars per individual complainant in some cases. Settlements have been equally

enormous. But increasing the dollar amount of monetary judgments does not equate to healing the spiritual injuries suffered by the complainant. The complainant, therefore, may be left with no resolution of the sense of fear that the respondent can continue to harm others. The monetary judgment doesn't deliver an affirmation that the church or the individual respondent will act with integrity in the future. In that event, the costs of civil litigation might very well outweigh the benefits for the complainant and the church. The complainant will not have had his or her trust in the church restored. The church's reputation in the community may have suffered severe damage that diminishes its ability to continue in ministry. Finally, the monetary judgment or settlement may be large enough to ruin the financial health of the church, thereby forcing its closure. Church leaders who underestimate the likelihood that their congregation will be involved in litigation also tend to underestimate the amount of insurance coverage that they realistically need. The result can be that a jury hands down a final verdict of liability in an amount that far exceeds the insurance coverage available, leaving the church with an obligation it may not have ready resources to pay. The trustees of United Methodist local churches are required by provisions in *The Book of Discipline* to annually review the adequacy of the property, liability, and crime insurance coverage on church-owned property, buildings, personnel and equipment for the purpose of ensuring that the church is adequately protected against risks. (*The Book of Discipline*, Nashville: United Methodist Publishing House, 2008, Paragraph 2532.2, page 722)

Building Best Practices for Ministry

The ability to make good ethical decisions as a professional in ministry is, I believe, an ability that can be developed and strengthened. It is not a skill that we are automatically equipped with simply because we are clergy. There are many tools that individuals and congregations can use to strengthen the professional's ability to make right ethical decisions and to lead the congregation in this regard. In this chapter, we will look at several helpful elements in the development of these best practices.

Individuals' Best Practices

Work Habits

Creating solid work habits is a good place to start. This would include establishing a regular schedule for work and a regular time for leisure. We all realize that the idea of a "regular" schedule in ministry sometimes seems impossible! A minister once said, "If I didn't have so many interruptions from people who need my assistance, I would be able to get my work done a lot faster!" Her colleague replied, "Maybe so, but I think those who are the interruptions are the reasons we come to work." Well spoken! However,

Notes:

whether we are dealing with interruptions or checking items off our "to do" lists, we would serve ourselves and our parishioners well by setting up a schedule and communicating it to everyone. We also need to communicate our regularly scheduled time off and how emergencies will be handled when we are unavailable. Let everyone know if Friday is your day off. Let everyone know how to contact you, or someone else on the church staff, in the event of an emergency. Then, follow the schedule and the plans for communication. Failures in this area lead to anxiety, at the least, and sometimes anger and distrust.

I once heard of a church that received a new pastor who lived in a distant community and didn't feel it was necessary to keep a regular weekday schedule at the church. The church secretary didn't know how to respond when parishioners called to speak to the pastor and he wasn't at the church, or even in town, except to take messages for him. People began to wonder if the pastor really was committed to their congregation. Eventually, complaints began to come to the members of the church council about the pastor's failure to keep some semblance of a regular schedule at the church during the week. The church council addressed the complaints by working with the pastor to establish a weekday schedule during which he would regularly be present at the church. They also developed a communication plan that would be followed when a parishioner needed to reach the pastor in an emergency. All of this was communicated to the entire congregation in a variety of media—the church bulletin, the website, the newsletter, and others—in a multi-faceted effort to reduce the anxiety among the members. The truth is that many of the complaints and much of the anxiety might have been prevented if either of two things had happened when the pastor first began at the church. First, if the church council had communicated to the pastor that there was an established weekday schedule which he would be expected to adhere to,

CLEAR COMMUNICATION
among leaders is crucial.

then he would have had a better understanding of the congregation's expectations from the beginning. Second, in the event no schedule expectations were shared with him, he could have established a regular weekday schedule for himself and shared it with everyone. By setting up a schedule and being present regularly, the pastor would have visibly and physically demonstrated his desire to be a part of the church.

Time Off

The concept of "time off" for a minister can be difficult. Do we think of time off as our Sabbath time, or leisure time, or something else? When my adult Bible study class considered the commandment to remember the Sabbath and keep it holy, they asked me this question: is leading the congregation in worship on Sundays work for the minister and if so, then when is Sabbath for the minister? My experience is that each minister must answer this for herself. Then, develop habits that allow you to guard and protect a time of rest each week. I know one minister who gives three hours of each day to physical exercise (her favorite exercise is running) and devotional reading instead of setting aside one day per week. I know a clergy couple who sets aside one evening a month for dinner and fellowship with another couple with whom they have been friends since seminary days. I know a minister who plays golf once or twice a month with a group of friends. Each of these ministers approaches time off and Sabbath a little bit differently from the others. The important point is that each of them pays attention to taking time for rest and fellowship. By following these habits, each of them is modeling best practices for stewardship of their health for themselves, their families, and their parishioners.

Health Care: Exercise and Nutrition

Along with good work habits and taking regular time for

Notes:

Notes:

Sabbath, another set of best practices involves exercise and nutrition habits. Many of the ministers I know are now enrolled in health insurance programs that reward proactive and preventive behaviors. Some of the recommended practices are as simple as walking every day for thirty minutes and eating lots of fruits and vegetables. Others include getting annual physical checkups, getting preventive screenings for high blood pressure, heart disease, diabetes, and cancer, and following your medical provider's advice. Good exercise and nutrition practices obviously provide direct health benefits to each individual. These types of best practices also provide excellent leadership for our congregations by modeling good stewardship of health to our parishioners.

Here is an example of the direct benefits to an individual and of the benefits for a congregation when one minister decided to follow his medical provider's suggested best practices for exercise and nutrition. Last year, Rev. Goodnature, went for his annual physical exam. His weight was up about fifteen pounds. His blood pressure was in the category his doctor described as "borderline high" and his cholesterol level was elevated. He reported that the most regular exercise he got was mowing the lawn once a week. His family history included diabetes and cancer in his closest relatives. Rev. Goodnature's medical provider said it was time to get serious about taking care of himself. He recommended daily physical exercise, and a prescription medication to control the blood pressure. Rev. Goodnature was reluctant to take the prescription, but he was willing to exercise more. He and his medical provider agreed that he would give exercise a try for a short time and then they would reevaluate his weight and his blood pressure. Rev. Goodnature's church has a parish nurse and he pledged to have his blood pressure checked regularly.

Rev. Goodnature got a comfortable pair of walking shoes and a pedometer. He started with a goal of walking thirty minutes every evening after work. It didn't take long for him to realize that many evenings he didn't get home until it was too dark to walk outside for thirty minutes. He began to take a walk around the church for a short midmorning break and another walk around the church at lunch time. Both he and his wife began making an effort to get home earlier so they could walk together in the evenings. Making the effort to walk together meant that they got home early enough to have dinner together too. That led to eating healthier meals at home. As you might hope, Rev. Goodnature began to notice that his clothes seemed to be fitting better. At the end of three months, he returned to the medical provider's office to have his blood pressure and his weight checked. He had lost ten pounds and his blood pressure was slightly improved. They agreed that he would keep up the exercise for three more months. A year has passed and Rev. Goodnature has continued walking every day and paying attention to what he eats. He has lost forty pounds, his blood pressure reading is normal, and his cholesterol levels are well within the normal range. He reports that he sleeps better and feels more energetic. At the church, other staff members have followed his lead and are taking walking breaks. There is a friendly competition going on to see who can walk the most steps each week! Parishioners have noticed his weight loss and consulted with the parish nurse to find out how they could follow his example. Rev.Goodnature's efforts to be a good steward of his own individual health have had very good results for him, for his family, and for his congregation.

Rev. Goodnature's adoption of better exercise and nutrition practices for himself required a measure of self discipline. We make decisions every day that either contribute to good stewardship of our health or detract from good stewardship of our health. Sustaining this self discipline over time contributes to our physical well being and strengthens our discipline in other areas including our work habits.

Notes:

Shared Best Practices

There is another set of good habits and best practices that we as ministers are well advised to include in our repertoire. These include regular times for sharing in study, fellowship, even counseling with our ministerial colleagues. The minister who must lead worship and preach a sermon every week knows how much time is involved in preparing for these responsibilities. You also know the wealth of resources available to support your preparations. Nolan B. Harmon, retired bishop of the United Methodist Church and author of *Ministerial Ethics and Etiquette* (Nashville:, Abingdon Press, 1987) provided excellent advice for the development of strong study habits, including keeping a regular study schedule and building a library of theological, devotional, and biblical resources. Today, almost all ministers have access to a new plethora of library resources through the internet. There are internet sites that provide "sermon starters", "sermon illustrations", even complete sermons that can for a price simply be printed out and delivered from the pulpit! Bishop Harmon also noted that ministerial fellowship groups provide a place in which to share ideas, see Scriptures from other perspectives, and form friendships with colleagues who are not necessarily in the same congregation as ours. In my experience, clergy covenant groups in which a small group of colleagues agrees to study and share together, can provide the group members with fresh ideas and renewed enthusiasm for the tasks of leadership. While individual study and preparation is an absolute necessity, participation in a study group that affords opportunities for conversation and fellowship can be equally as beneficial.

Covenant Study Groups

You may ask why the clergy covenant study group is included here as a best practice worth engaging in. What does such a group have to contribute to our abilities to make good decisions regarding professional leadership? We gain new insight through sharing our questions, our dilemmas, and our ideas with our peers. When we are new or inexperienced in some responsibilities, we can learn from others who have faced similar situations. When we have been engaged in ministry for a longer time, we can be inspired by the perspectives of newer members of the study group. Participating in a fellowship study group in which the members honor each other by preparing for the study and by participating regularly affords us opportunities for seeking guidance or sharing guidance with others. It is possible to graduate from seminary without completing a formal course in professional ethics and ethical decision-making. However, ministers can, within covenant study groups, acquire the concepts and framework for making good decisions through sharing their questions and experiences with each other. The list of topics for examination in covenant study groups need not be limited to the lectionary and sermon ideas. I would encourage the group to explore a wide variety of topics and issues such as financial leadership of the congregation, Christian Education leadership, personnel policies and procedures, evangelism and marketing strategies, and many others. For example, sharing conversation in the group on the meaning of the clergy-penitent confidentiality and privilege in light of your state's child abuse reporting statute and Paragraph 341.5 of *The Book of Discipline* would be helpful for all group members who have children or youth in their congregations. The group's exploration of the requirements of the reporting statute along with an examination of the ways to protect the children from injury can strengthen each member's understanding of some very important responsibilities of ministry. As my dad would say, we can learn some things from books, some things from experience, and some things from each other. Covenant study groups provide us opportunity for learning in all these ways.

Notes:

Perhaps the most profound value of participation in covenant study groups is that our participation prevents us from becoming isolated in our individual silo of stress. As congregational leaders we may not think it is advisable to freely develop collegial relationships or close friendships with parishioners so as not to develop problematic dual relationships. However, we must not let ourselves become so wrapped up in our tasks that we don't make time for nurturing friendships and strong collegial bonds for ourselves with others. Isolation can lead us to depression, ineffectiveness, and increasing stress. Poor decision-making can often grow out of this type of isolation and leads to serious consequences such as boundary violations in personal or professional relationships.

In addition, there are a huge number of internet sites commonly referred to as "social networking sites" which make opportunities for online "conversation" available to groups of individuals. Usually, the participants in a network share some common interests or concerns. There are networks populated by ministers sharing interests in preaching, or kayaking, and nearly any other topic. The numbers of persons and groups connecting in these networking sites grows exponentially every day. Perhaps some illustrations of the numbers would be helpful. The websites known as Google, Facebook, and Twitter are widely-known sites. A recent report in *Time* (Steven Johnson, June 15, 2009, "How Twitter Will Change the Way We Live") states that during the month of April, 2009, Google had more than one hundred million visitors, Facebook had more than seventy million visitors, and Twitter had more than seventeen million visitors. All of these websites had large increases in the number of visitors between 2008 and 2009. Additionally, each visitor to a website might make multiple "searches" or connections. In "Did You Know?", the YouTube video produced by Jeff Brenman, Karl Fisch, and Scott McLeod, it is said that more than thirty billion searches are conducted on Google each month. It is also reported that there are two hundred million registered users of the social networking site known as MySpace—a number that would exceed the entire population of Brazil. "Did You Know?" reports that one of every eight couples married last year met online. In contrast, attorneys and judges are anecdotally reporting that online abuses, such as online pornography, are the most frequently cited reasons for divorces.

It is beyond the scope of this resource to engage is an exhaustive discussion of the uses and purposes of websites and technology for creating social connections among persons. However, it is important for us as ministers to understand the pervasiveness of technological networking in our congregations and communities. We recognize that these types of connections may give us new informational resources. We must also recognize that these connections might not provide us with relationships that can support us and connect us in ways that will prevent a growing trend of isolation and distance from each other either professionally or personally. Our parishioners need to come to the same kind of realizations about the benefits and costs of technological social connections. We must work to achieve a reasonable balance between our participation in online networks and our participation in personal covenant communities.

Clergy Care: Counseling

Another shared best practice for us as ministers is counseling—either in a group setting or in a setting that includes a counselor and a counselee. Ministers are often comfortable acting as the counselor but uncomfortable seeking counseling for themselves. We can ably articulate the benefits of counseling for our parishioners or our peers but we seem reluctant to seek the same benefits for ourselves. When we find ourselves feeling over-anxious, or too stressed to be able to make good decisions, then consultation with a competent counselor can

Notes:

Notes:

provide us with new insights and tools for reducing the stress and making better decisions. I have known a few ministers who believed strongly in the benefit of a counseling relationship for themselves. Each time they move into a new community they intentionally seek out a counselor and engage in a professional relationship with him or her even before any crisis arises. Entering into the counseling relationship can offer the minister an opportunity to work out stressful issues without placing undue pressure on friends or spouses and thereby minimize the difficulties of dual relationships.

Conclusion

Building trust between ministers and their parishioners is of paramount importance for the church's mission and ministry. When parishioners act by always putting the best interests of the church ahead of their individual preferences, the mission is advanced. When ministers act with integrity, always acknowledging their responsibilities to the congregation, trust between minister and parishioners will certainly be nurtured. In our world, the ethical leadership of ministers is needed in congregations, communities, and our entire society. Ministers who are skillful counselors, astute administrators, and inspirational preachers are hoped for by every church. This study resource is, hopefully, a practical guide for each minister seeking to develop decision making and leadership skills. We have explored a variety of the elements that go into creating Safe Sanctuaries® in our congregations through leadership in areas such as financial analysis, Christian education, counseling relationships, and visitation. While the study contained here can be completed by an individual minister, a greater benefit will be derived by study together with other colleagues in ministry and with congregational leaders who can expand the individual understandings and expectations.

INTEGRITY IS BUILT ON discipline, accountability, and resonsibility.

Every day, nearly, brings another call to my desk reporting the latest failure of leadership of a professional in ministry. Last week, the reports concerned persons who were pastors, teachers, and music ministers. At the end of every week, I pray that next week will bring reports of ministry that was enhanced and protected because a minister and a congregation planned in advance and built policies and procedural structures in advance that would support the mission of the gospel of Jesus Christ. I confess that some weeks are better than others! I'm encouraged by the growing recognition in ministers and in congregations that if trust and integrity are presupposed in the pastoral relationships, then trust and integrity must be nurtured, supported, and honored in every circumstance by parishioners and ministers alike. Discipline, accountability, and responsibility will all be needed to strengthen our leadership and to enliven our community. We can be comforted by the knowledge that we do not have to lead or work alone. We have answered the call into Christian community. We can find peers, colleagues, and friends with whom to share the mission and ministry. We can build our congregations into Safe Sanctuaries® equipped for making disciples of Christ for the transformation of the world! Our work will surely be rewarded.

Notes:

Bibliography and Resources

Bakke, Dennis W. *Joy at Work*. Seattle, WA: PVG, 2005.

Bloss, Julie L., J.D. *The Church Guide to Employment Law, 2nd Edition*. Matthews, NC: CMR Press, 1999.

The Book of Discipline of the United Methodist Church 2008. Nashville: The United Methodist Publishing House, 2008.

Conflict and Communion, Nashville: Discipleship Resources, 2006.

Coles, Robert. *Living Lives of Moral Leadership*. New York: Random House, 2000.

Covey, Stephen R. *The 8th Habit*. New York: FREE PRESS division of Simon & Schuster, Inc., 2004.

Crabtree, Jack. *Better Safe than Sued*. Loveland, CO: Group Publishing, Inc., 1998.

Fortune, Marie. *A Sacred Trust*. Seattle: FaithTrust Institute, 2005.

Fowler, James W. *Faithful Change*. Nashville: Abingdon Press, 1996.

Gaede, Beth Ann, Editor. *When a Congregation is Betrayed*. Herndon, VA: Alban Institute, 2006.

Hamilton, Adam. *Enough*. Nashville: Abingdon Press, 2009.

Hammar, R., Ed. *Church Law and Tax Report*. Carol Stream, IL: Christianity Today.

Harmon, Nolan B. *Ministerial Ethics and Etiquette*. Nashville: Abingdon Press, 1987.

The Holy Bible, NRSV. Nashville: Thomas Nelson Publishers, 1989.

Hopkins, Nancy Myer and Mark Laser, Editors. *Restoring the Soul of a Church*. Collegeville, MN: The Liturgical Press, 1995.

Logan, Mary, J.D. *The Buck Stops Here*. Nashville: Discipleship Resources, 1998.

McClintock, Karen A. *Preventing Sexual Abuse in Congregations*. Herndon, VA: Alban Institute, 2004.

Mount, Jr., Eric. *Professional Ethics in Context*. Louisville: Westminster/John Knox Press, 1990.

Outler, Albert, ed. *The Work of John Wesley, vol. 1*. Nashville: Abingdon Press, 1984.

Rediger, G. Lloyd. *Clergy Killers*. Louisville: Westminster John Knox Press, 1997.

Salter, Anna C., Ph.D. *Predators, Pedophiles, Rapists, and Other Sex Offenders*. Specialized Training Services, 2003. Video.

———. *Truth, Lies, and Sex Offenders*. New York: Basic Books, 2003.

Shakespeare, William. *Othello, The Moor of Venice*.

Willimon, W. H. *Calling and Character*. Nashville: Abingdon Press, 2000.